4TH Edition

BEST ⛺ TENT
Camping

WISCONSIN

YOUR CAR-CAMPING GUIDE TO SCENIC BEAUTY, THE SOUNDS OF NATURE, AND AN ESCAPE FROM CIVILIZATION

T0125823

This book is for Ellie Connolly,
who loves the Wisconsin outdoors. —JM

Best Tent Camping: Wisconsin

Published by Menasha Ridge Press
Distributed by Publishers Group West
Manufactured in China
Fourth edition, fourth printing 2024

Library of Congress Cataloging-in-Publication Data

Names: Revolinski, Kevin, author. | Molloy, Johnny, 1961– author.
Title: Best tent camping Wisconsin : your car-camping guide to scenic beauty, the sounds of nature, and an escape
   from civilization / Kevin Revolinski and Johnny Molloy.
Description: 4th edition. | Birmingham, Alabama : Menasha Ridge Press, 2018. | Includes index.
Identifiers: LCCN 2017044128| ISBN 9781634041430 (pbk.) | ISBN 9781634041447 (ebook)
   ISBN 9781634042062 (cloth)
Subjects: LCSH: Camping—Wisconsin—Guidebooks. | Camp sites, facilities, etc.—Wisconsin—Guidebooks. |
   Wisconsin—Guidebooks.
Classification: LCC GV191.42.W6 R486 2018 | DDC 796.5409775—dc23
LC record available at https://lccn.loc.gov/2017044128

Cover and interior design: Jonathan Norberg
Maps: Steve Jones
Project editor: Holly Cross
Copy editor: Kerry Smith
Proofreader: Emily Beaumont
Indexing: Rich Carlson

MENASHA RIDGE PRESS

An imprint of AdventureKEEN
2204 First Ave. S., Ste. 102
Birmingham, AL 35233

Visit menasharidge.com for a complete listing of our books and for ordering information. Contact us at our website, at
facebook.com/menasharidge, or at twitter.com/menasharidge with questions or comments. To find out more about
who we are and what we're doing, visit blog.menasharidge.com.

Front cover: Main photo: Amnicon Falls State Park (see page 86) by Dale Kittleson
Inset photo: Bear Lake Campground (see page 129) courtesy of the U.S. Forest Service/public domain

4TH Edition

BEST TENT Camping

WISCONSIN

YOUR CAR-CAMPING GUIDE TO SCENIC BEAUTY, THE SOUNDS OF NATURE, AND AN ESCAPE FROM CIVILIZATION

Kevin Revolinski
& Johnny Molloy

MENASHA RIDGE PRESS
Your Guide to the Outdoors Since 1982

Wisconsin Campground Locator Map

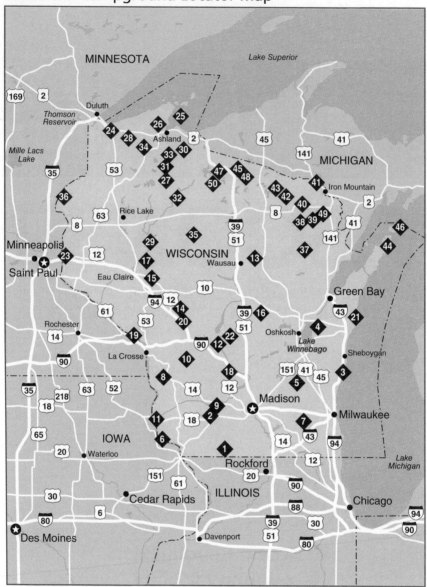

CONTENTS

NORTHWESTERN WISCONSIN 85

NORTHEASTERN WISCONSIN 125

Map Legend

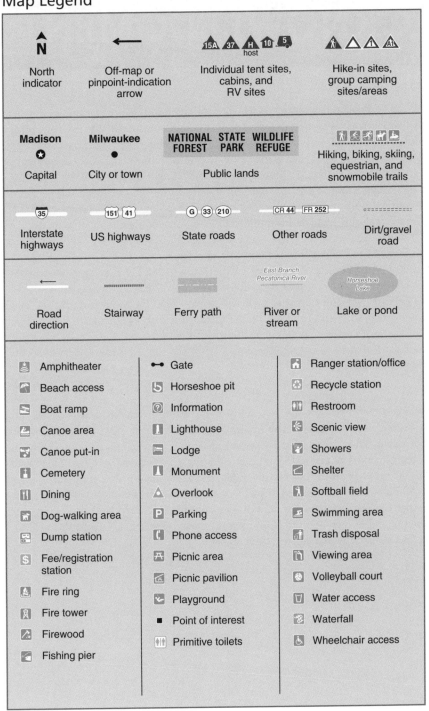

N North indicator	← Off-map or pinpoint-indication arrow	Individual tent sites, cabins, and RV sites	Hike-in sites, group camping sites/areas
Madison ✪ Capital	**Milwaukee** ● City or town	**NATIONAL STATE WILDLIFE FOREST PARK REFUGE** Public lands	Hiking, biking, skiing, equestrian, and snowmobile trails
35 Interstate highways	**151 41** US highways	**G 33 210** State roads	**CR 44 FR 252** Other roads ═══ Dirt/gravel road
← Road direction	Stairway	Ferry path	*East Branch Pecatonica River* River or stream — *Horseshoe Lake* Lake or pond

Amphitheater
Beach access
Boat ramp
Canoe area
Canoe put-in
Cemetery
Dining
Dog-walking area
Dump station
Fee/registration station
Fire ring
Fire tower
Firewood
Fishing pier

Gate
Horseshoe pit
Information
Lighthouse
Lodge
Monument
Overlook
Parking
Phone access
Picnic area
Picnic pavilion
Playground
Point of interest
Primitive toilets

Ranger station/office
Recycle station
Restroom
Scenic view
Showers
Shelter
Softball field
Swimming area
Trash disposal
Viewing area
Volleyball court
Water access
Waterfall
Wheelchair access

ACKNOWLEDGMENTS

I would like to thank the following people for helping me in the research and writing of this book: all the land managers of Wisconsin's state parks and forests, the folks at Chequamegon-Nicolet National Forest, and the people who administer the many county parks throughout the state. Specifically I would like to thank Ron Campbell, Niki Robinson, Melissa Parker, and B. J. Farra at Wildcat Mountain State Park; Pat and Cindy Hummer at Wildcat Mountain; Brian Hefty, Paul Ahlen, and Barry Fetting of Hartman Creek for their captivating commentary; Geoffrey Cooke and Garrett Meador at Rock Island State Park; Scott Johnson and Neal Kephart at Wyalusing State Park; and Jim and Paul Volz and their families at Starrett Lake. Thanks also to P. Lynn, Amp I. Tay, Bruce, and Melinda at White Deer Lake; and to Darin Williams and Allen Middendorp of Lake Wissota State Park.

Thanks to Ellie Connolly for canoeing with me on the St. Croix and for advising me on her favorite tent-camping destinations. Thanks to Jackie White for her help too. Thanks to Linda Grebe at Eureka! for providing me with a great tent, the Mountain Pass 2X. Thanks to Silva for their compasses and to Camp Trails for their packs. Thanks to Jean Cobb and Brooke Wilson at Freebairn & Company for their help.

The biggest thanks of all go to the people of Wisconsin, who have a beautiful state in which to tent camp.

—Johnny

Wisconsinites need to know just how marvelous a park system we have—not just on the state level but also the national, county, and even city/village levels. I thank all the people who work each day to maintain these parks and serve and protect those of us who come to visit them. No one is getting rich out there, and for many it is a labor of love. Volunteers and "friends of" the park groups are indispensable in keeping these places as they are. I am also grateful for all those who donated or sold land for the purposes of these wild natural places rather than development, and the activists who, out of love for the land, worked so hard to find the funding or legislation to make many of these places exist. Thanks above all to my father, for teaching me to love the outdoors.

—Kevin

PREFACE

Welcome to the fourth edition of *Best Tent Camping: Wisconsin.* In seeking new tent-camping destinations, I teamed up with Madison resident Kevin Revolinski, who loves all things Wisconsin. And certainly the outdoors is one of the state's finer things. Globe-trotting Kevin always returns from his travels more appreciative of the vast wildlands in his home state, and he has eagerly added his knowledge and talent to this book. Plus, he's a good guy and has an authentic Wisconsin accent.

It is such a privilege to improve and update yet another edition of this Wisconsin tent-camping guide. Life is so interesting—you just never know where it will lead you. I certainly would not have known just how unique and beautiful Wisconsin is if it weren't for serendipitous fortune. Way back when, I met Tom Rodgers, who was moving from Madison, Wisconsin, to Knoxville, Tennessee, to further the college teaching career of his wife, Kathleen. He waxed eloquent about the beauty of the Badger State. I had been stopping in Wisconsin some on trips, but I hadn't explored it fully. Tom introduced me to his friend Ellie Connolly, who talked up Wisconsin even more. Then the opportunity arose to write this book. I grabbed my tent and laptop and hopped in my auto, exploring the state by day and typing up on-site campground reports by night.

The first surprise came at Wyalusing State Park. The view from the bluffs of the Wisconsin River rivaled any mountain vista, as did views from the walk-in tent sites at Nelson Dewey State Park. Big lakes border parts of the Badger State, so I went to enjoy the cool breezes at Point Beach State Forest, on the shores of Lake Michigan. The tan sand squished beneath my toes as I looked up at Rawley Point Lighthouse. In the central part of the state were two of the biggest surprises of all, Dells of the Eau Claire and Hartman Creek. Hartman Creek is an exemplary state park: an attractive, relaxing campground with lots of nearby natural features to enjoy. The Dells of the Eau Claire, a county park east of Wausau, is a rocky natural feature on the Eau Claire River that is a must for all those who want to know their state well. Speaking of rocks, have you seen the view from the top of Roche-A-Cri? That is one amazing natural feature, with a nice campground within walking distance. More bluffs waited at Perrot State Park, astride the Mississippi River.

And then there are the Northwoods. It seems that tent campers from Wisconsin and points beyond like to go "up Nort," as it is often said. And there are so many fine campgrounds up north—it was difficult to choose the best. Not only are there many state parks but also county parks, state forests, and national forests. Two common themes to the campgrounds of the Northwoods are water and natural beauty, from Big Bay State Park in the Apostle Islands of Lake Superior, to Amnicon Falls in Douglas County, to serene Laura Lake, where the loons provided the background music to those long, long summer days. And I can't forget the fantastic rivers of the Northwoods, the Bois Brule, the Flambeau, and the Peshtigo, as well as the Namekagon. But singling out the Northwoods rivers would leave out many fine paddling rivers throughout the state. Wisconsin is paddling country—from the East Fork Pecatonica down south, to the Black River of the central region, and to the federally preserved St. Croix astride the Minnesota border. And there are still other rivers—the wild lower Wisconsin, the Kickapoo, the Chippewa, and the Eau Claire near the city of Eau Claire. Campgrounds in this book are along or near all the above rivers.

The days began to shorten—fall was on its way as I explored more campgrounds. And with the joy of completing a book and the sadness of an adventure ended, I finished my research. But I have since continued putting my lessons to work, enjoying more of Wisconsin in outdoor adventures, including a 230-mile, 15-night canoe trip down the Namekagon and St. Croix Rivers.

Kevin and I continue to explore and enjoy more of the Badger State. The two of us have not only patrolled the campgrounds but have also explored its hiking trails and rivers, writing about them. So whether you are at one of the tent campgrounds described in this book, on a scenic river, or on a rewarding hiking trail, don't be surprised if you run into Kevin or me! In the meantime, happy tent camping in Wisconsin.

—Johnny

A NOTE ABOUT STATE PARK & FOREST FEES

Wisconsin State Park and State Forest campgrounds have seasonal pricing, the highest price, of course, being for summer camping, during which time there is also a price increase for Friday and Saturday nights. The period of May 1 to the Thursday before Memorial Day Weekend and from Labor Day to October 31 are considered Spring/Fall and are commonly a few dollars cheaper and without weekend rates. Winter, of course, is the cheapest option. The prices listed in this guide are based on summer season weekends. Also note there is a two-night minimum for high season when reserving in advance.

—Kevin & Johnny

BEST CAMPGROUNDS

BEST FOR HISTORY

BEST FOR PADDLING

BEST FOR PRIVACY

BEST FOR QUIET

BEST FOR SPACIOUSNESS

BEST FOR SECURITY

BEST FOR WHEELCHAIRS

You'll find excellent hiking near North Trout Lake Campground (see page 150).

INTRODUCTION

HOW TO USE THIS GUIDEBOOK

Menasha Ridge Press welcomes you to *Best Tent Camping: Wisconsin.* Whether you are new to this activity or have been sleeping in your portable outdoor shelter during decades of outdoor adventures, please review the following information. It explains how we have worked with the authors to organize this book and how you can make the best use of it.

THE RATING SYSTEM

As with all books in the Best Tent Camping series, the authors personally experienced dozens of campgrounds and campsites to select the top 50 locations in Wisconson. Within that universe of 50 sites, the authors then ranked each campground according to the six categories described below.

Each campground is superlative in its own way. For example, a site may be rated only one star in one category but perhaps five stars in another category. Our rating system allows you to choose your destination based on the attributes that are most important to you. Although these ratings are subjective, they're still excellent guidelines for finding the perfect camping experience for you and your companions.

★★★★★   The site is **ideal** in that category.

★★★★   The site is **exemplary** in that category.

★★★   The site is **very good** in that category.

★★   The site is **above average** in that category.

★   The site is **acceptable** in that category.

BEAUTY

In the best campgrounds, the fluid shapes and elements of nature—flora, water, land, and sky—have melded to create locales that seem to have been made for tent camping. The best sites are so attractive that you may be tempted not to leave your outdoor home. A little site work is all right to make the scenic area camper friendly, but too many reminders of civilization eliminated many a campground from inclusion in this book.

PRIVACY

A little understory goes a long way in making you feel comfortable once you've picked your site for the night. There is a trend in planting natural borders between campsites if the borders don't exist already. With some trees or brush to define the sites, everyone has his or her personal space. Then you can go about the pleasures of tent camping without keeping up with the Joneses at the site next door—or them with you.

SPACIOUSNESS

This attribute can be very important depending on how much of a gearhead you are and the size of your group. Campers with family-style tents and screen shelters need a large, flat spot on which to pitch a tent with more room for the ice chest to prepare foods, all the while not getting burned near the fire ring. We just want enough room to keep our bedroom, den, and kitchen separate.

QUIET

The music of the lakes, rivers, and all the land between—the singing birds, rushing streams, waves lapping against the shoreline, wind whooshing through the trees—includes the kinds of noises tent campers associate with being in Wisconsin. In concert, they camouflage the sounds you don't want to hear—autos coming and going, loud neighbors, and so on. Criteria for this rating include several touchstones: the authors' experience at the site, the nearness of roads, the proximity of towns and cities, the probable number of recreational vehicles (RVs), the likelihood of noisy all-terrain vehicles (ATVs) or boats, and whether a campground host is available or willing to enforce the quiet hours. Of course, one set of noisy neighbors can deflate a five-star rating into a one-star (or no-star), so the latter criterion—campground enforcement—was particularly important in the authors' evaluations of this category.

SECURITY

How you determine a campground's security will depend on who you view as the greater risk: other people or the wilderness. The more remote the campground, the less likely you are to run into opportunistic crime, but the more remote the campground, the harder it is to get help in case of an accident or dangerous wildlife confrontation. A remote campground with no civilization nearby is usually safe, but don't tempt potential thieves by leaving your valuables out for all to see. Campground hosts are wonderful to have around, and state parks with locked gates are ideal for security. Get to know your neighbors and develop a buddy system to watch each other's belongings when possible.

Ratings in this category take into consideration whether there was a campground host or resident park ranger, proximity of other campers' sites, how much day traffic the campground received, how close the campground was to a town or city, and whether there was cell-phone reception or some type of pay phone or emergency call button.

CLEANLINESS

We're sticklers for this one. Nothing will sabotage a scenic campground like trash. Most of the campgrounds in this guidebook are clean. More rustic campgrounds—our favorites—usually receive less maintenance. Busy weekends and holidays will show their effects; however, don't let a little litter spoil your good time. Help clean up, and think of it as doing your part for Wisconsin's natural environment.

A campground's appearance often depends on who was there right before you and how your visit coincides with the maintenance schedule. In general, higher marks went to those campgrounds with hosts who cleaned up regularly. The rare case of odor-free toilets also gleaned high marks. At campgrounds without a host, criteria included trash receptacles and evidence that sites were cleared and that signs and buildings were kept repaired. Markdowns for the campground were not given for a single visitor's garbage left at a site, but old trash in the shrubbery and along trails, indicating infrequent cleaning, did secure low ratings.

THE CAMPGROUND PROFILE

Each profile contains a concise but informative narrative of the campground and individual sites. Not only is the property described, but readers can also get a general idea of the recreational opportunities available in the area and perhaps suggestions for touristy activities. This descriptive text is enhanced with three helpful sidebars: Ratings, Key Information, and Getting There (accurate driving directions that lead you to the campground from the nearest major roadway).

THE CAMPGROUND LOCATOR MAP AND MAP LEGEND

Use the locator map on page iv to pinpoint the location of each campground. The campground's number follows it throughout this guidebook: from the locator map, to the table of contents, and to the profile's first page. This book is organized by region, as indicated in the table of contents.

A map legend that details the symbols found on the campground-layout maps appears immediately following the Table of Contents, on page vii.

CAMPGROUND-LAYOUT MAPS

Each profile contains a detailed map of individual campsites, internal roads, facilities, and other key elements.

GPS CAMPGROUND-ENTRANCE COORDINATES

Readers can easily access all campgrounds in this book by using the directions given and the overview map, which shows at least one major road leading into the area. But for those who enjoy using GPS technology to navigate, the book includes coordinates for each campground's entrance in latitude and longitude, expressed in degrees and decimal minutes.

To convert GPS coordinates from degrees, minutes, and seconds to the above degree decimal-minute format, the seconds are divided by 60. For more on GPS technology, visit usgs.gov.

A note of caution: A dedicated GPS unit will easily guide you to any of these campgrounds, but users of smartphone mapping apps may find that cell service is often unavailable in the remote areas where many of these hideaways are located.

ABOUT THIS BOOK

In preparing the fourth edition of this book, Kevin Revolinski and I roamed the Badger State reviewing campgrounds. In addition to our on-site inspections, we also updated all pertinent information, such as campground fees, phone numbers, and websites.

The two of us hope you will enjoy this updated book, for Wisconsin is rich in both human and natural history. Wisconsin was originally settled by aboriginal Americans who used the ample rivers and lakes for travel. French voyageurs and United States pioneers followed, exploring a land shaped by glaciers and time. Green Bay and Prairie du Chien were settled first, as furs, lead, and lumber attracted more settlers. The vast and varied landscape was evident to all who came to the area. They saw the sand dune–laden shores of Lake Michigan, the lake-studded highlands of the Northwoods, the ridges and valleys of the southwest where the Wisconsin and Mississippi Rivers cut deep swaths through the land, and the deep gorges cut by dark, fast-flowing rivers forming waterfalls spilling into Lake Superior.

Today, tent campers can enjoy these parcels, each distinct regions of Wisconsin. You can explore the surprisingly hilly terrain of Sidie Hollow, near the Illinois border. The bluffs of Perrot State Park overlook Minnesota. The central region features the remote and wild Black River State Forest, where timber wolves have reclaimed their old domain, with the quiet of East Fork Campground returning you to nature. Here also are the big waters of Castle Rock Flowage, where Buckhorn's numerous walk-in tent-camping sites await. A tent camper has to take two ferries to reach Rock Island State Park, Wisconsin's most northeastern point. So many lakes dot Wisconsin's Northwoods that you can literally camp on two lakes at once, such as Birch Grove Campground in the Chequamegon-Nicolet National Forest or Luna–White Deer Lake Campground in the Nicolet National Forest. And then there are the waterfalls of the Northwoods. Marinette County calls itself the waterfall capital of Wisconsin. Two campgrounds in this book are situated along falls in Marinette County, with many other cascades nearby. Yet more falls are featured at other parks in this book.

All this spells paradise for the tent camper. No matter where you go, the scenery will never fail to please the eye. Before embarking on a trip, take time to prepare. Many of the best tent campgrounds are a fair distance from the civilized world, and you want to enjoy yourself rather than make supply runs. Call ahead and ask for a park map, brochure, or other information to help you plan your trip. Visit the campground's website. Make reservations wherever applicable, especially at popular state parks. Inquire about the latest reservation fees and entrance fees at state parks and forests.

Ask questions . . . and more questions. The more questions you ask, the fewer surprises you will get. There are other times, however, when you'll grab your gear and this book, hop in the car, and just wing it. This can be an adventure in its own right.

WEATHER

Spring is the most variable season. During March, you'll find your first signs of rebirth in southern Wisconsin, yet trees in the Northwoods may not be fully leafed out until June. Both winter- and summerlike weather can be experienced in spring. As summer approaches, the strong fronts weaken, and thunderstorms and haze become more frequent. Summertime rainy days can be cool. In fall, continental fronts once again sweep through, clearing the air and bringing warm days and cool nights, though rain is always possible. The first snows of winter usually arrive in November, and snow can fall intermittently through April. About 40–120 inches of snow can fall during this time. Expect to incur entire days of below-freezing weather, though temperatures can range from mild to bitterly cold.

FIRST AID KIT

A typical first aid kit may contain more items than you might think necessary. These are just the basics. Prepackaged kits in waterproof bags (Atwater Carey and Adventure Medical make a variety of kits) are available. As a preventive measure, take along sunscreen and insect repellent. Even though quite a few items are listed here, they pack down into a small space.

- Adhesive bandages, such as Band-Aids

- Antibiotic ointment (Neosporin or the generic equivalent)

- Antiseptic or disinfectant, such as Betadine or hydrogen peroxide

- Aspirin, acetaminophen (Tylenol), or ibuprofen (Advil)
- Benadryl or the generic equivalent, diphenhydramine (in case of allergic reactions)
- Butterfly-closure bandages
- Comb and tweezers (for removing ticks from your skin)
- Epinephrine in a prefilled syringe (for people known to have severe allergic reactions to such things as bee stings)
- Gauze (one roll and six 4-by-4-inch compress pads)
- LED flashlight or headlamp
- Matches or lighter
- Moist towelettes
- Moleskin/Spenco 2nd Skin
- Pocketknife or multipurpose tool
- Waterproof first aid tape
- Whistle (for signaling rescuers if you get lost or hurt)

ANIMAL AND PLANT HAZARDS

BLACK BEARS

There are more than 30,000 black bears in Wisconsin. Adults are 4–6 feet in length, making them the largest mammal after elk. Their primary range is the upper third of the state; their secondary range is in a band across the central third, and occasional sightings have been reported as far south as the Wisconsin River Valley in Sauk County.

Black bears are timid and solitary by nature, so it is unlikely you will see one. They are most active at twilight and April–November. Bears are generally afraid of people and usually are the first to flee when they sense that a person is near. A female bear can become aggressive when it has a cub, however, and should always be avoided. Never run from a bear, just back away slowly.

In Wisconsin bears are most often attracted by garbage. Don't leave food out when not in use. Store it in a bear-resistant storage unit or car trunk. Use bear-resistant trash receptacles in parks that have them. Don't sleep in clothes you cooked in, and keep pets on a leash. All this said, the threat is quite minimal.

MOSQUITOES

Although it's not a common occurrence, individuals can become infected with the West Nile virus by being bitten by an infected mosquito. Culex mosquitoes, the primary varieties that can transmit West Nile virus to humans, thrive in urban rather than natural areas. They lay their eggs in stagnant water and can breed in any standing water that remains for more than five days. Most people infected with West Nile virus have no symptoms of illness, but some may become ill, usually 3–15 days after being bitten.

In Wisconsin, summer is thought to be the highest risk period for West Nile virus. At this time of year—and anytime you expect mosquitoes to be buzzing around—you may want to wear protective clothing, such as long sleeves, long pants, and socks. Loose-fitting, light-colored clothing is best. Spray clothing with insect repellent. Remember to follow the instructions on the repellent and to take extra care with children.

TICKS

Ticks like to hang out in the brush that grows around campsites and along trails. Hot summer months seem to explode their numbers, but you should be tick-aware during all months of the year. Ticks, which are arachnids and not insects, need a host to feast on to reproduce. The ticks that light onto you will be very small, sometimes so tiny that you won't be able to spot them. Primarily of two varieties, deer ticks and dog ticks, both need a few hours of actual attachment before they can transmit any disease they may harbor. Ticks may settle in shoes, socks, or hats, and they may take several hours to actually latch on. The best strategy is to visually check yourself a couple of times a day, especially if you've gone out for a walk in the woods. Ticks that haven't attached are easily removed but not easily killed. If you pick off a tick in the woods, just toss it aside. If you find one on your body at camp, you may want to dispatch it (otherwise it may find you again). For ticks that have embedded, removal with tweezers is best.

EMERALD ASH BORER

The emerald ash borer (*Agrilus planipennis*) is an exotic insect native to Asia that currently threatens ash trees in the Great Lakes region. The pest can be spread inadvertently in infested firewood, and most parks have strict rules about what wood you can bring into the park. By following some simple rules, you can help prevent the spread of these destructive insects. Purchase aged firewood near your campsite location; don't bring it from home. Almost all parks offer firewood at reasonable prices, and wood is often available from private sellers just outside the parks. Firewood purchased at or near your destination should be used during your camping trip; don't take any to another destination. Buy wood that has no bark or loose bark (a sign the wood is very dry). This will reduce the chances of infestation while also making your fire easier to start.

photographed by Tom Watson

POISON IVY, POISON OAK, AND POISON SUMAC

Recognizing poison ivy, oak, and sumac and avoiding contact with them is the most effective way to prevent the painful, itchy rashes associated with these plants. Poison ivy *(left)* ranges from a thick, tree-hugging vine to a shaded ground cover, three leaflets to a leaf; poison oak *(see next page)* occurs as either a vine or shrub, with three leaflets as well; and poison sumac flourishes in swampland, each leaf containing 7–13 leaflets. Urushiol, the oil in the sap of these plants, is responsible for the rash. Usually within 12–14 hours of exposure (but sometimes much later), raised lines and/or blisters will appear, accompanied by a terrible itch. Refrain from scratching because bacteria under fingernails can cause infection and you will spread the rash to other parts of your body. Wash and dry the rash thoroughly,

photographed by Jane Huber

applying a calamine lotion or other product to help dry the rash. If itching or blistering is severe, seek medical attention. Remember that oil-contaminated clothes, pets, or hiking gear can easily cause an irritating rash on you or someone else, so wash not only any exposed parts of your body but also clothes, gear, and pets.

TIPS FOR A HAPPY CAMPING TRIP

Few things are more disappointing than a bad camping trip, especially since it is so easy to have a great one. To assist with making your outing a happy one, here are some pointers:

- **GO ONLINE OR CALL AHEAD WHENEVER POSSIBLE.** This way you can familiarize yourself with the area. If traveling to the Chequamegon-Nicolet National Forest, order a forest map online. Not only will a map make it that much easier to reach your destination, but nearby hikes, scenic drives, waterfalls, and landmarks will also be easier to find. Once you arrive at your destination, ask questions. Most stewards of the land are proud of their piece of terra firma and are honored you came for a visit. They're happy to help you have the best time possible.

- **RESERVE YOUR SITE IN ADVANCE.** Do this when it's an option, especially if it's a weekend or a holiday, or if the campground is wildly popular. Many prime campgrounds require at least a 6-month lead time on reservations. Check before you go.

- **PICK YOUR CAMPING BUDDIES WISELY.** A family trip is pretty straightforward, but you may want to reconsider including grumpy Uncle Fred who does not like bugs, sunshine, or marshmallows. After you know who is going, make sure that everyone is on the same page regarding expectations of difficulty, sleeping arrangements, and food requirements.

- **DON'T DUPLICATE EQUIPMENT.** You only need so many cooking pots and lanterns among campers in your party. Carry what you need to have a good time, but don't turn the trip into a major moving experience.

- **DRESS FOR THE SEASON.** Educate yourself on the temperature highs and lows of the specific area you plan to visit. It may be warm at night in the summer in your backyard, but up in the Northwoods it may be quite chilly.

- **PITCH YOUR TENT ON A LEVEL SURFACE.** Try to find one that is covered with leaves, pine straw, or grass. Pitch your tent on a tarp or specially designed footprint to thwart ground moisture and to protect the tent floor. Do a little site maintenance, such as picking up small rocks and sticks that can damage your tent floor and make sleep uncomfortable. If you have a separate tent rainfly but don't need it, keep it rolled up at the base of the tent in case it starts raining at midnight.

- **TAKE A SLEEPING PAD WITH YOU.** Take one that is full length and thicker than you think you might need. This will not only keep your hips from aching on hard ground but will also help keep you warm. Don't forget a pillow!

- **PLAN TASTY MEALS.** If you are not hiking to a primitive campsite, there is no need to skimp on food due to weight. Bring everything you will need to prepare, cook, eat, and clean up the mess.

- **IF YOU'RE PRONE TO USING THE BATHROOM MULTIPLE TIMES AT NIGHT, PLAN AHEAD.** Leaving a warm sleeping bag and stumbling around in the dark to find the restroom—whether it is an outhouse, a fully plumbed facility, or just the woods—is no fun. Keep a flashlight and any other accoutrements you may need by the tent door, and know exactly where to head in the dark. For guys, a practical (but often scoffed) solution is to keep a wide-mouth Nalgene-type bottle in the tent and use that inside the sleeping bag at night. Be discreet, though, and dispose of the night's work appropriately.

- **STANDING DEAD TREES AND STORM-DAMAGED LIVING TREES CAN POSE A REAL HAZARD TO TENT CAMPERS.** These trees may have loose or broken limbs that could fall at any time. When choosing a backcountry campsite or a spot to rest, look up.

CAMPING ETIQUETTE

Camping experiences can vary wildly depending on a variety of factors, such as weather, preparedness, fellow campers, and time of year. Here are a few tips on how to create good vibes with fellow campers and wildlife you encounter.

- **OBTAIN ALL PERMITS AND AUTHORIZATION AS REQUIRED.** Make sure you check in, pay your fee, and mark your site as directed. Don't make the mistake of grabbing a seemingly empty site that looks more appealing than your site. It could be reserved. If you are unhappy with the site you've selected, check with the campground host for other options.

- **LEAVE ONLY FOOTPRINTS.** Be sensitive to the ground beneath you. Be sure to place all garbage in designated receptacles, or pack it out if none is available. No one likes to see the trash someone else has left behind.

- **NEVER SPOOK ANIMALS.** It's common for animals to wander through camp-sites, where they may be accustomed to the presence of humans (and our food). An unannounced approach, a sudden movement, or a loud noise startles most animals. A surprised animal can be dangerous to you, to others, and to themselves. Give them plenty of space.

- **PLAN AHEAD.** Know your equipment, your ability, and the area in which you are camping—and prepare accordingly. Be self-sufficient at all times; carry necessary supplies for changes in weather or other conditions. A well-executed trip is a satisfaction to you and to others.

- **BE COURTEOUS TO OTHER CAMPERS.** This includes hikers, bikers, and others you encounter.

- **STRICTLY FOLLOW THE CAMPGROUND'S RULES REGARDING THE BUILDING OF FIRES.** Never burn trash. Trash smoke smells horrible, and trash debris in a fire pit or grill is unsightly.

BACKCOUNTRY CAMPING ADVICE

A permit is not required before entering the backcountry to camp. However, you should practice low-impact camping. Adhere to the adages "Pack it in; pack it out" and "Take only pictures; leave only footprints." Practice "leave no trace" camping ethics while in the backcountry.

Open fires are permitted except during dry times, when the forest service may issue a fire ban. Backpacking stoves are strongly encouraged. You are required to hang your food (so bears and other animals can't get to it) to minimize human impact on wildlife and avoid their introduction to and dependence on human food. Wildlife learns to associate backpacks and backpackers with easy food sources, thereby influencing their behavior. Make sure you have about 40 feet of thin but sturdy rope to properly secure your food. Ideally, you should throw your rope over a stout limb that extends 10 or more feet aboveground. Make sure that the rope hangs at least 5 feet away from the tree trunk.

Solid human waste must be buried in a hole at least 3 inches deep and at least 200 feet away from trails and water sources; a trowel is basic backpacking equipment.

Following the above guidelines will increase your chances for a pleasant, safe, and low-impact interaction with nature.

VENTURING AWAY FROM THE CAMPGROUND

If you go for a hike, bike ride, or other excursion into the boondocks, here are some tips:

- **ALWAYS CARRY FOOD AND WATER.** Do this whether you are planning to go overnight or not. Food will give you energy, help keep you warm, and sustain you in an emergency situation until help arrives. You never know if you will have a stream nearby when you become thirsty. Bring potable water or treat water before drinking it from a stream. Boil or filter all found water before drinking it.

- **STAY ON DESIGNATED TRAILS.** Most hikers get lost when they leave the path. Even on the most clearly marked trails, there is usually a point where you have to stop and consider which direction to head. If you become disoriented, don't panic. As soon as you think you may be off-track, stop, assess your current direction, and then retrace your steps back to the point where you went awry. If you become absolutely unsure of how to continue, return to your vehicle the way you came in. Should you become completely lost and have no idea of how to return to the trailhead, remaining in place along the trail and waiting for help is most often the best option for adults and always the best option for children.

- **BE ESPECIALLY CAREFUL WHEN CROSSING STREAMS.** Whether you are fording the stream or crossing on a log, make every step count. If you have any doubt about maintaining your balance on a foot log, go ahead and ford the stream instead. When fording a stream, use a trekking pole or stout stick for balance and face upstream as you cross. If a stream seems too deep to ford, turn back. Whatever is on the other side is not worth risking your life.

- **BE CAREFUL AT OVERLOOKS.** While these areas may provide spectacular views, they are potentially hazardous. Stay back from the edge of outcrops and be absolutely sure of your footing; a misstep can mean a nasty and possibly fatal fall.

- **KNOW THE SYMPTOMS OF HYPOTHERMIA.** Shivering and forgetfulness are the two most common indicators of this insipid killer. Hypothermia can occur at any elevation, even in the summer, especially when the hiker is wearing lightweight cotton clothing. If symptoms arise, get the victim shelter, hot liquids, and dry clothes or a dry sleeping bag.

- **TAKE ALONG YOUR BRAIN.** A cool, calculating mind is the single most important piece of equipment you'll ever need on the trail. Think before you act. Watch your step. Plan ahead. Avoiding accidents before they happen is the best recipe for a rewarding and relaxing hike.

In writing this book, we had the pleasure of meeting many friendly, helpful people: local residents proud of the unique lands around them, as well as state park and national forest employees who endured endless questions. Even better were fellow tent campers, who were eager to share knowledge about their favorite spots. They already know what beauty lies on the horizon. As this state becomes more populated, these lands become that much more precious. Enjoy them, protect them, and use them wisely.

SOUTHERN
WISCONSIN

photographed by Kevin Revolinski

A short, scenic trail leads to Stephens Falls in Governor Dodge State Park (see page 15).

1

Blackhawk Memorial Park Campground

Beauty ★★★ / Privacy ★★★★★ / Spaciousness ★★★★★ / Quiet ★★★★ / Security ★★★ / Cleanliness ★★★

This quiet county park on the East Branch Pecatonica River is sure to have an open campsite.

Blackhawk Memorial Park isn't exactly the most publicized place around, and yet it is on both the National and Wisconsin Registers of Historic Places. This Lafayette County park, located on the small but canoeable East Branch Pecatonica River, contrasts mightily with ultrabusy Yellowstone Lake State Park, which lies a few miles upstream in the Pecatonica River watershed. The only way you might find out about this quiet park is by word of mouth, or maybe from a curious guidebook writer on the lookout for the best tent-camping destinations in Wisconsin. And yes, Blackhawk Memorial Park is one of the best. Here, you can camp along the river in a very large, secluded campground. Once here, you can do a little canoeing, fishing, and relaxing, or you can visit Yellowstone Lake, and then return to your quiet retreat. You might even paddle the Pecatonica proper, which flows through nearby Darlington.

The access road rolls through farmland and then dips into the East Branch Pecatonica Valley as it approaches the park. Just beyond the entrance, you will pass a shelter, a water spigot, and restrooms. Beyond that point, campsites are spread all over the place amid

Canoeists enjoy the Pecatonica River.

photographed by Kevin Revolinski

KEY INFORMATION

CONTACT: Lafayette County Sportsman Club Alliance, 608-465-3472

OPEN: Year-round; roads not plowed in winter

SITES: 36

EACH SITE: Fire pit, most have picnic table

ASSIGNMENT: First come, first served

REGISTRATION: Self-registration on-site

FACILITIES: Vault toilets, water spigots

PARKING: At campsites only

FEE: Monday–Thursday, $5/vehicle; Friday–Sunday, $10/vehicle

ELEVATION: 800'

RESTRICTIONS:

PETS: On leash only

FIRES: In fire pit only

ALCOHOL: At campsites only

VEHICLES: No restrictions

grassy areas broken by coppices of trees and wooded wetlands. Solitude and spaciousness prevail in this little-used locale. Horseshoe Lake lies below to your left. The road ahead divides. The right fork leads to the upper canoe landing on the East Branch Pecatonica and a small grassy flat, where four secluded campsites are set against a line of trees along the river. The left fork leads to another camping area near the Dead River, a small lake that was once part of the East Branch of the Pecatonica.

The park is also known as Bloody Lake—site of a battle between militiamen and the Sauk and Fox tribes—and is recorded in the National Register as the Pecatonica Battlefield. In 1832, Black Hawk, the leader of the Sauk and Fox tribes, tried to reclaim his treaty-ceded land near the site of present-day Rock Island, Illinois. He was unsuccessful and, as a result, fled to Wisconsin while being pursued by the militia. There were numerous battles along the way (one of which is memorialized by a plaque at site 14), but on June 16, 1832, Black Hawk and his followers were defeated near Bad Axe Creek, Wisconsin, not far from the Mississippi River.

Follow the road to reach several shaded sites by the still waters. The campground road curves onward toward two coveted sites, 15 and 16, on the shore of pretty Horseshoe Lake. Return to the East Branch Pecatonica River, a good bit downstream of the upper landing. Here, the lower canoe landing is set amid several open sites along the riverbank. Reach a couple of secluded shady sites, 31 and 32, and then curve away from the river back to the shore of Bloody Lake, across from the Blackhawk Memorial. This campground road curves more than a snake climbing a tree. A few other well-separated, well-scattered sites are on Bloody Lake.

Want to camp on a holiday weekend? Come here, and a site should be available. Want privacy? This is the place. Want a big site? Look no farther. However, the wooded marshes and lakes here create ripe conditions for mosquitoes—be prepared mid-May–June and on through to fall. The fishing here is purportedly good: walleye, bass, panfish, and a few northern pike are in the river. Paddlers can float the East Branch Pecatonica from Argyle down to the campground, or downstream toward South Wayne and the main Pecatonica River. The main Pecatonica offers paddling opportunities of its own, especially from Darlington downstream. Make a gentle float past woods, prairielands, and farm country. You will also see bluffs and rock outcrops. Darlington is so proud of the paddling opportunities here that they hold a canoe festival the second week of June! Also in Darlington is the

Cheese Country Trail, a 47-mile rail-trail corridor leading from Mineral Point to Monroe. You could combine a float down the river with a bike trip. Call 608-776-5706 for more info on the rail-trail.

The very small and quiet hamlet of Woodford is just a mile to the south of Blackhawk. If you are looking for some busy outdoor action, head to Yellowstone Lake State Park, north of Argyle. The 450-acre Yellowstone Lake is the park centerpiece. The state park offers fishing, swimming, and boating, and it has 10 miles of hiking trails. After your visit to Yellowstone, you will be glad that everyone else hasn't heard about Blackhawk Memorial.

Blackhawk Memorial Park Campground

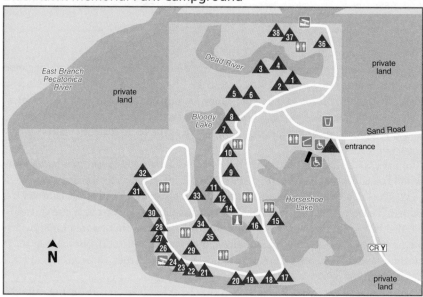

GETTING THERE

From Argyle, take WI 81 east 2.5 miles to Trotter Road. Turn right on Trotter Road and follow it 2.5 miles to a T intersection. Turn right, staying on Trotter Road 1 mile to Sand Road. Stay straight on Sand Road (Trotter Road veers left) and follow it 1 mile to the park, on your right.

GPS COORDINATES: N42° 39.687' W89° 52.658'

2

Governor Dodge State Park Campgrounds

Beauty ★★★★ / Privacy ★★★ / Spaciousness ★★★★ / Quiet ★★★ / Security ★★★★ / Cleanliness ★★★★

You aren't the only one to find this an excellent place to camp. Archaeological evidence puts humans here more than 8,000 years ago.

About 450 million years ago, this region of Wisconsin was all under the sea, and the sediment deposited at that time built up the colorful layers of sandstone that peek out through the forest covering on many of the hills. Wind and water erosion shaped the land thereafter, but the glaciers of the most recent ice age remarkably passed this region over. Whereas the sheet of ice thousands of feet thick leveled the land in many directions, this area was untouched, and the result is hills and valleys in the otherwise flat plains of the surrounding geography.

You aren't the only one to find this an excellent place to camp. Archaeological evidence puts humans here more than 8,000 years ago. The park takes its name from General Henry Dodge, the first territorial governor of Wisconsin. When immigrants from Europe arrived to mine lead in the 1820s, conflicts arose between them and the native Winnebago people who were already working the mines. Dodge was a key figure in bringing peace between the two groups.

Explore almost 40 miles of hiking trails at Governor Dodge State Park   *courtesy of Shutterstock*

KEY INFORMATION

CONTACT: Wisconsin Department of Natural Resources, 608-935-2315, tinyurl.com/governordodge; reservations 888-WI-PARKS, wisconsin.goingtocamp.com

OPEN: Year-round

SITES: 189 primitive, 80 electric, 6 backpack

EACH SITE: Picnic table, fire ring, gravel parking pad

ASSIGNMENT: By phone; internet; or first come, first served

REGISTRATION: At park office

FACILITIES: Showers, flush toilets, pit toilets, water spigot, pay phones

PARKING: At campsites only

FEE: Wisconsin residents, $20 ($30 electric site); nonresidents, $35 ($35 electric site); plus vehicle admission fee (Wisconsin residents, $8; nonresidents, $11; Wisconsin residents age 65 and older, $3); $7.75 reservation fee

ELEVATION: 1,242'

RESTRICTIONS:

PETS: On leash only, except in designated pet swimming areas

FIRES: In fire ring only; firewood must be purchased in state within 25 miles of campground

ALCOHOL: At campsites and picnic areas

VEHICLES: 2/site

OTHER: Quiet hours 11 p.m.–8 a.m.

This park encompasses 5,270 acres of varying hills, valleys, forests, and prairies. White-tailed deer, wild turkeys, grouse, and foxes are common, and more than 150 species of birds have been identified here. Two man-made lakes—Twin Valley and Cox Hollow, the results of earthen dams across Mill Creek—rest within the park's boundaries.

For each lake there is a corresponding campground. From the park office, follow the curving road into the forest and along Cox Hollow Lake to arrive at Cox Hollow Campground, which is divided into two sections—wooded and open sites. When you enter the camping section, follow the road to the left to the wooded section, which features tall oak-hickory and maple trees. The first sites on the left, sites 5 and 6, are specifically for tents and have a bit more seclusion than the others along the first strip. A small parking area and a short trail serve each. Keep driving to the center of this section to find playground equipment and the showers and restrooms. Sites 16–20 are less private and closer together down the center of this roughly figure eight layout. Head down to the far side of the campground to sites 21, 22, 24, and 32, which each offer a view through the foliage of the lake below. They are situated near the cliff's edge, but don't worry—a safety fence keeps kids or sleepwalkers from wandering too close. Sites 27, 29, and 30 are on top of a bluff and lose the lake view but are nevertheless beautiful. Avoid sites 37–41, which are less private and tighter together, albeit closer to the restrooms.

Sites with a number above 100 are grassy, open sites located in the section to the right as you enter the campground. These are less private from the road but are separated quite nicely from neighbors by substantial brush. Site 111 is the best one of this group, and a short trail to it provides the seclusion that the others lack. These sites are better spread out than the wooded sites, and though they are less shaded, many still have at least one or two tall trees. Sites up the middle road are the least private, are closer to facilities, and are geared more toward families.

From the entrance to Cox Hollow Campground, head north and the road will open up to a prairie. Turn right on the road to Twin Valley Campground—this is clearly marked.

Twin Valley is also divided into wooded and open sites. Most of these sites offer electricity, and the RVs will gravitate here. An absence of brush like that found at Cox Hollow means that you can see your neighbors. Open sites are 300–356. Avoid sites 306, 307, and 309, as they offer no privacy. Overall, Twin Valley really doesn't compare to Cox Hollow. Despite that, the six best sites in the park are here. Tent sites 262–264 and 269–271 are a 50- to 100-foot walk into the woods on the far eastern loop of the wooded sites. They are nicely spread out and quite private. Parking is available at the trailhead for each group of three sites.

Six backpack sites are also available and are up a trail 0.5 mile from the parking lot in the Hickory Ridge Group Camp Area, situated in the far northeast corner of the park. Pit toilets and water for these sites are at the parking area as well.

Reservations are available up to 11 months in advance. Sites in Cox Hollow are open for dates beginning the first Thursday of May; site availability ends the second Wednesday of October (for sites 2–48) or the day after Labor Day (for sites 49–118). Sites in Twin Valley are open for reservations May 1–late October. Backpacker sites accept reservations from April 1. At least 30 sites in the Twin Valley Campground remain open in winter, and a few of them are plowed. Drinking water is available at the park office during this time.

Bring your bike and enjoy the 12 miles of off-road biking trails. These connect up to the 40-mile Military Ridge State Trail, which goes all the way to Madison and requires a trail pass. Each lake has a swimming area and changing facilities with vending machines, and anglers will find bass, walleye, muskie, and panfish.

Hiking trails total almost 40 miles, including passes through both forest and prairie, and more than 150 species of birds have been identified inside the park. But the critters you want to be wary of are the raccoons at night: Pack your supplies carefully!

Governor Dodge State Park Campgrounds

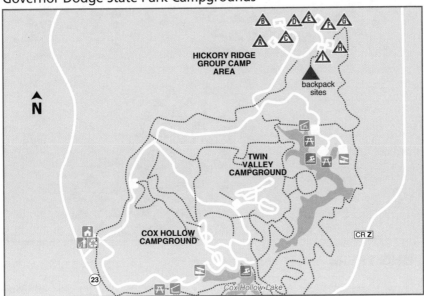

Governor Dodge State Park: Cox Hollow Campground

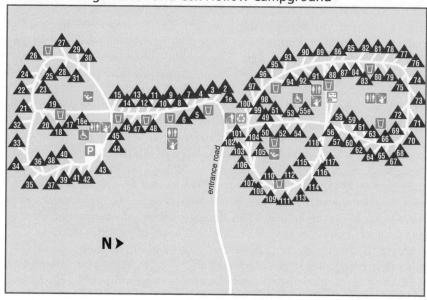

Governor Dodge State Park: Twin Valley Campground

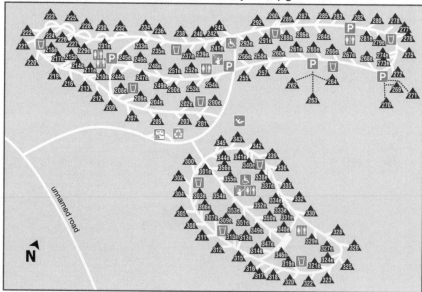

GETTING THERE

From Dodgeville, head north out of town on WI 23. Just 3 miles out you will find the park entrance on the right.

GPS COORDINATES: N43° 00.977' W90° 08.484'

3

Harrington Beach State Park Campground

Beauty ★★★★ / Privacy ★★★ / Spaciousness ★★★★ / Quiet ★★★ / Security ★★★★ / Cleanliness ★★★★★

Camp a short hike away from one of the most accessible public beaches along Lake Michigan, a short drive from Milwaukee.

With its marvelous beaches along Lake Michigan and easy hiking trails, Harrington Beach State Park is quite popular with families and day-trippers. The park has some of the best sandy beaches so close to Milwaukee. On summer weekends you will see a lot of families coming here with the kids. But this wasn't always a recreational site. From the late 19th century up until 1925, limestone was quarried here. A historical walking trail passes some scattered ruins of what was Stonehaven, a mining company town. The quarry is now a small lake surrounded by nicely shaded hiking trails. The beach is quite a hike from the campsites, and the beach parking lot often fills up fast. But campers can use a shuttle that loops through the park all day until 7 p.m.

The campgrounds, which were only added in 2009, are comprised of two loops that lie farther inland and south from the beach area. The North Loop is where you will find the

A short trail encircles Quarry Lake.   *photographed by Kevin Revolinski*

KEY INFORMATION

CONTACT: Wisconsin Department of Natural Resources, 262-285-3015, tinyurl.com/harringtonbeach; reservations 888-WI-PARKS, wisconsin.goingtocamp.com

OPEN: First Wednesday in May–last weekend in October

SITES: 33 primitive, 31 electric, 5 walk-in

EACH SITE: Picnic table, fire ring

ASSIGNMENT: By phone; internet; or first come, first served

REGISTRATION: At park attendant station

FACILITIES: Hot showers, flush toilets, vault toilets, water spigots, laundry

PARKING: At campsites or overflow lot

FEE: Wisconsin residents, $20 ($32 electric site); nonresidents, $25 ($37 electric site); plus vehicle admission fee (Wisconsin residents, $8; nonresidents, $11; Wisconsin residents age 65 and older, $3); $7.75 reservation fee

ELEVATION: 600'

RESTRICTIONS:

PETS: On leash only

FIRES: In fire ring only; firewood must be purchased in state within 25 miles of campground

ALCOHOL: At campsites only

VEHICLES: 2/site

OTHER: 14-day stay limit

---

sites with electricity. As you enter the loop, it is a one-way ride through a crossroad, passing the campground host site on your right before choosing which direction on the loop you want to go. While separation between campers is good with lots of intervening brush, the trees are still young and shade is minimal. Exceptions include sites 119, 120, and 121, which are more shaded and grown in and have electric hookups. A short trail to the shuttle pickup lies between sites 123 and 124.

The South Loop is the better of the two and is just slightly more spread out, with its southern half running oblong east to west. Sites are still quite open and sunny but separated nicely and staggered so that you are not facing the neighbor across the road. Site 207 has nice shade trees, as do sites 212–216 and 220. For a bit more privacy, consider sites 226 and 227.

The real winning sites here for privacy are the walk-in sites. The trail to them leaves from the parking lot across from the shower building and goes through a meadow. Sites W1 and W2 offer the best shade, but W3–W5 are farther apart from each other and farther from the rest of the campground. One more campsite just off the beach is reserved exclusively for kayakers paddling along Lake Michigan. You can park at Kohler-Andrae State Park to the north or at the marina in Port Washington.

The hiking trails are short and easy, including a 0.5-mile nature trail through a white cedar swamp, as well as a short loop around Quarry Lake. Birders come for great migration numbers on the lake and a nice chance to see hawks en masse on their route. Stargazers also get a bonus here: Northern Cross Science Foundation (ncsf.info) maintains the Jim and Gwen Plunkett Observatory with its 2,000-pound, 20-inch telescope. Check their website to see their schedule of free public viewings.

Harrington Beach State Park Campground

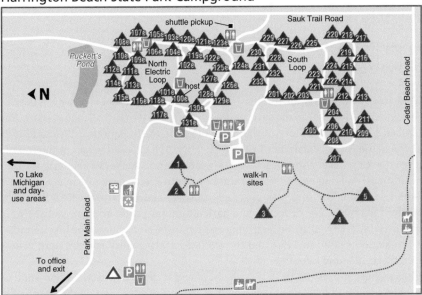

GETTING THERE

From I-43, take Exit 107 (Belgium/Lake Church) and go east on County Road D about 1 mile. The park entrance will be on your right.

GPS COORDINATES: N43° 29.630' W87° 48.135'

4

⚠ High Cliff State Park Campground

Beauty ★★★★ / Privacy ★★ / Spaciousness ★★★ / Quiet ★★★ / Security ★★★ / Cleanliness ★★★

Camp atop the edge of the Niagara Escarpment with nice views of Lake Winnebago below.

Here's a state park with a lot to offer: the state's largest internal lake with a beach and marina, a stellar long view of the surrounding counties, easy and challenging hikes, American Indian history, and a story of the big geology of North America. Welcome to High Cliff! The name is the centerpiece of the rock story. The exposed ledges at the top of this bluff overlooking Lake Winnebago are the westernmost reaches of the Niagara Escarpment. It's hard to imagine, but at one time this entire ledge was nearly deforested by a limekiln operation. The rock was quarried, crushed, and kilned right here before being shipped off for roads, construction, and agricultural purposes. You can still see ruins of the industrial site, as well as the quarrying and deposits, along one of the hiking trails. The lime production ceased in 1956, and the affiliated 19th-century general store is now an interpretive center and museum.

The campground sits on the top of the bluff and is divided into two loops—one north (right) and one south (left)—each with a crossroad full of sites running the length of it. At

Check out the limekiln ruins while hiking at High Cliff.

photographed by Kevin Revolinski

the entrance to the campground are a playground, small amphitheater, and showers. All sites are well shaded by maple, oak, and hickory trees. Sites 1–3 are spaced out with 50 feet in between, but you can still see each other. Otherwise, sites are separated by some understory and staggered so that you don't look directly at the campers across the road. The trailhead to the Indian Mound Trail and its five effigies lies right across from site 17.

The cliff-side Red Bird Trail runs along the west end of the campground, right behind sites along the back rows of either loop; these include sites 22–25, 38, 39, 68, 70, 87, 88, 90, and 91. When the leaves are in the trees, there really isn't much of a view of the lake from there, but there is some interesting exposed dolomite. Sites 39 and 40 straddle that trailhead and offer a bit of sunshine through the canopy. Sites 53–112 are in the southern loop and offer thicker brush between sites for more privacy, and another entrance to the Red Bird Trail appears between sites 87 and 88. Sites 70–74 offer electricity. Just beyond the tree cover behind the southernmost row of sites (evens 92–98, odds 99–109) is an open prairie. Double sites, better for larger groups, include 6–9, 14–15, 22–25, and electric sites 110–111. The camp host has site 58.

The smokestack of a historical limekiln

photographed by Kevin Revolinski

The park fills up on weekends in summer, and the electric sites generally go first. Primitive camping is allowed in winter but moves to the group camp area, and no water service is offered. Cross-country ski trails get a lot of use at that time, and some park roads become trails.

The hiking trails are all loops of varying skill levels, and you can see the 12-foot bronze statue of Winnebago chief Red Bird along the trail that takes his name. This particular trail skirts the edges of the cliffs (mind the small children!) and offers intermittent lake views. But the best view is at the park's highest point from an observation tower there. Access to the lake includes a beach area and a marina. Pets are not allowed here, but there is a designated pet picnic area within the park.

High Cliff State Park Campground

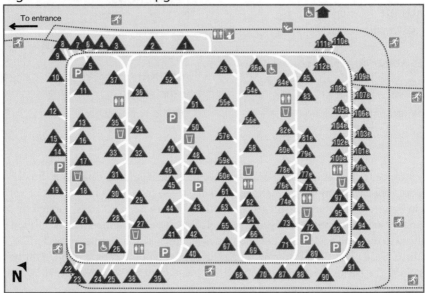

GETTING THERE

From US 41 in Neenah, take WI 114 east just about 10 miles to Pigeon Road. Take Pigeon Road almost 2 miles south and go south (left) where it ends at Lower Cliff Road. Follow this 1,000 feet to the park entrance on your right.

GPS COORDINATES: N44° 10.025' W88° 17.477'

5

Ledge County Park Campground

Beauty ★★★ / Privacy ★★ / Spaciousness ★★★★ / Quiet ★★★ / Security ★★★ / Cleanliness ★★★★

Camp under the tall oaks and maples at this campground that overlooks wildlife-rich Horicon Marsh.

Ledge County Park is named for the Horicon Ledge, a western extension of the Niagara Escarpment, the same ancient rock formation over which Niagara Falls flows. In this case, the escarpment is a wooded hilltop bordered with rock bluffs that overlook Horicon Marsh and the surrounding countryside. At 32,000 acres, Horicon Marsh is the largest freshwater cattail marsh in the country. The marsh is situated along the Canada geese flyway, with 200,000 birds passing through in spring and fall. Many other creatures call the marsh home.

Ledge County Park makes for a good jumping-off point to explore both the ledges at the park and the marsh below. The campground, a little rough around the edges, has some good tent sites, as well as some electric sites that will make the case for why you are a tent camper. The tent sites have their own loop, and you will be satisfied calling this county park home for a night. But don't expect a bunch of sedate bird-watchers here. Your fellow tent campers are likely to be fun-loving families and others out to enjoy the warm days of summer.

Boardwalks allow up close exploration of Horicon Marsh.

photographed by Kevin Revolinski

KEY INFORMATION

CONTACT: Dodge County Parks, 920-386-3700 ext. 1, tinyurl.com/dodgeledgepark

OPEN: April–October

SITES: 21 primitive, 24 electric

EACH SITE: Picnic table, fire ring

ASSIGNMENT: By phone, internet, or first come, first served

REGISTRATION: At park attendant station

FACILITIES: Hot showers, flush toilets, vault toilets, water spigots

PARKING: At campsites only

FEE: $20 ($24 electric site)

ELEVATION: 950'

RESTRICTIONS:

PETS: On leash only

FIRES: In fire ring only; only use firewood purchased at park

ALCOHOL: At campsites only

VEHICLES: 2/site

OTHER: Quiet hours 10 p.m.–7 a.m.; 1 tent (6 people)/site (additional tent for children allowed; additional tents allowed with prior approval and extra fee)

Pass the office and enter the electric loop. Continue past campsites 1 and 2, which overlook a volleyball court and a field beyond. Climb a hill and pass by a string of campsites with electricity; these sites are shaded but too close together, with nothing but grass and dirt between them. The best aspect of the electric loop is the kid's playground. The good loop, the nonelectric loop, spurs off to the right. Tall oaks and maples shade the hillside. Last year's leaves carpet the campsites. These sites are lettered A–U. If you are going to reserve a site here, ask for a letter site. Sites A and B are behind one another. C–J are strung along the road well away from one another, with young trees adding campsite privacy. Campsite E is all alone. A miniloop houses sites K, L, and M. The loop curves around toward the Horicon Ledge. Campsites N, O, P, T, and U are also backed against the ledge on the outside of the loop, while Q, R, and S are on the inside of the loop. Campsites 23 and 24 are closer to the ledge on a miniloop. All these sites are well shaded and suited for a tent.

The Ledge Rocks Trail runs along the escarpment, winding through woods and along rocks where you can see below. In places, boulders have fallen from the bluff, forming minicaves with trails going under and around them. In other places, paths lead from boulder to boulder, and hikers have to step over deep crevices to continue their journey. A virtual maze of trails connects the escarpment to another trail running along the bottom of the escarpment past the Contemplation Tree, a huge oak, and on to a spring. Other paths interconnect in the deep woods opposite the ledge. A handy trail map is available at the campground office.

Bird-watching from the deck overlooking Horicon Marsh

photographed by Kevin Revolinski

Now that you have seen the marsh from above, it's time to see it up close. The northern two-thirds of the marsh is a national wildlife refuge, while the southern portion is managed by the State of Wisconsin. Visit the Horicon Marsh International Education and Visitor Center, just north of the town of Horicon on WI 28. It has lots of interpretive information, a boardwalk, and nature trails. The lake levels of the flowage are regulated to enhance wildlife habitat. The visitor center overlooks Bachhuber Impoundment, while to the west, near the Department of Natural Resources Field Station on North Palmatory Road, a viewing platform looks out over the larger marsh and the Rock River. In the national refuge is another visitor center off WI 49, as well as a driving loop and more hiking trails and boardwalks. Bikers and hikers can also enjoy the Wild Goose State Trail. It follows an old rail corridor along the west side of Horicon Marsh for 34 miles between Juneau and Fond du Lac. The best place for campers to pick up the trail is at Minnesota Junction, 4 miles west of the campground off WI 33.

The waters of Horicon Marsh offer another way to see the preserve. Canoes are available for rent at Blue Heron Landing in Horicon. You may want to take a pontoon boat tour. A guide will lead the tour and dish out a lot of information. Birding tours are also offered. Call 920-485-4663 for information about Blue Heron offerings. After coming here, you will have seen two natural features that make Wisconsin so special.

Ledge County Park Campground

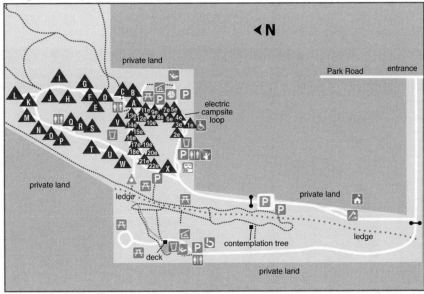

GETTING THERE

From the junction with US 41 in Allenton, take WI 33 west 13 miles to County Road V. Turn right on CR V and follow it 1 mile to Raasch's Hill Road. Turn left on Raasch's Hill Road and follow it 2 miles to Park Road, entering the park.

GPS COORDINATES: N43° 27.423' W88° 36.252'

6

⛺ Nelson Dewey State Park Campground

Beauty ★★★★★ / Privacy ★★★★★ / Spaciousness ★★★★ / Quiet ★★ / Security ★★★★★ / Cleanliness ★★★★

The views from the walk-in tent sites are among the best anywhere.

The campground is the star of this destination. It has most of the qualities that a tent camper desires: a not-too-big campground with widely spaced sites that are large with near maximum privacy, in an area that showcases a beautiful forest. And that's just the regular campground! Nelson Dewey also has four walk-in tent campsites that have all of the above plus ridgetop views of the Mississippi River and across to Iowa. In addition, this state park is blessed with amenities both within and nearby that will keep you busy when you are not standing around admiring your campsite.

Usually, any campground has a few dud sites. Not this one. By the way, all campsites here are reservable, so make your plans. The campground is set on a bluff line peering down on the Mississippi River. From the park entrance, follow the camp road to reach the camping loop on the left, situated beneath a cathedral-like hardwood forest dominated by oak

Visit Stonefield Historic Site, just across the road from Nelson Dewey State Park.

courtesy of the Wisconsin Historical Society

KEY INFORMATION

CONTACT: Wisconsin Department of Natural Resources, 608-725-5374, tinyurl.com/nelsondewey; reservations 888-WI-PARKS, wisconsin.goingtocamp.com

OPEN: Year-round; bathhouse and spigots open May–October; park roads are not plowed in winter

SITES: 23 primitive, 18 electric, 4 walk-in

EACH SITE: Picnic table, fire grate

ASSIGNMENT: By phone; internet; or first come, first served

REGISTRATION: At park office or self-registration if office is closed

FACILITIES: Hot showers, flush toilets, pit toilets, water spigots, carts for toting gear to campsites

PARKING: At campsites only

FEE: Wisconsin residents, $16 ($28 electric site); nonresidents, $21 ($33 electric site); plus vehicle admission fee (Wisconsin residents, $8; nonresidents, $11; Wisconsin residents age 65 and older, $3); $7.75 reservation fee

ELEVATION: 900'

RESTRICTIONS:

PETS: On leash only

FIRES: In fire ring only; firewood must be purchased in state within 25 miles of campground

ALCOHOL: At campsites only

VEHICLES: 2/site

OTHER: 14-day stay limit

---

trees. Younger trees and heavy brush form a privacy-delivering understory. Pass campsites 1 and 2. These large, shaded sites are typical of the campground. Campsite 3 is even larger. A vault toilet for both sexes is located past a double site. The Woodbine Nature Trail lies across the campground road. Pass a few electric sites, along with an all-access site, to reach a spur road leading left. You'll find a few electric sites as well as some real winners on this miniloop. Site 18 has a view of the river below. Site 17 sits all alone and is highly recommended. A short foot trail in between these two sites leads to the walk-in tent sites.

Handy pull carts are provided to transport your gear from your vehicle to the walk-in campsites. These bluff-side sites have been leveled with landscaping timbers. Walk-in site D is first. It offers a stunning view to the southeast and is partially shaded by locust trees. Site A offers an excellent view also and is more shaded. A portable toilet is located near site B. A final spur trail leads to site C, arguably the best of the best. It looks far to the southwest at the end of the ridgeline. Shade trees overhang the site. Be apprised that you can hear trains traveling the riverside tracks at the base of the bluff, whether you are at the walk-in sites or not. They didn't bother me a bit.

The main campground loop continues beyond the spur roads and circles past a modern bathhouse. It then reaches another spur loop housing sites 24–31. This is the domain of the electricity-loving big rigs and the only place a tent camper wouldn't want to be. But even these sites are attractive and would work just fine. Pass the firewood shed. A series of nonelectric sites graces the loop as it circles to an end. The large sites are very well separated.

This smallish state park offers some trails along the Mississippi River bluff. The Prairie Trail features rocky points with fantastic vistas of their own, and the Cedar Trail offers overlooks too. Once the home of Wisconsin's first governor, Nelson Dewey, the park preserves his home, which you can tour. Other than that, the park serves as a jumping-off point for nearby attractions. Just across the road is the Stonefield Historic Site, owned and operated by the Wisconsin Historical Society. Originally a farm started by Dewey, the area now includes the Wisconsin State Agricultural Museum and a 1900s village exhibit. The museum houses farm implements of the past and rare, one-of-a-kind machines. It also follows the history of farming in the Badger State. The turn-of the-19th-century exhibit features 30 reconstructed buildings displaying a small farm community from the early 1900s. Stonefield is open Memorial Day–mid-October.

Some campers will use private facilities in nearby Cassville to fish the Mississippi River. Kids will want to swim in the Cassville public pool, which charges a small fee. Consider canoeing or tubing the nearby Grant River, down by Beetown. It offers a quiet, scenic, small-river experience. A rental and shuttle service operates on the Grant during the warm season. For more information on the Grant River, call Grant River Canoe Rental at 608-794-2342.

Nelson Dewey State Park Campground

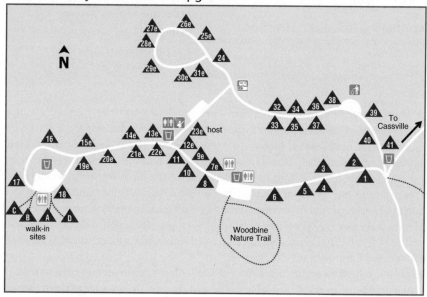

GETTING THERE

From downtown Cassville, head north on WI 133 for 0.5 mile to County Road VV. Turn left on CR VV and follow it 1.2 miles to the state park, on your right.

GPS COORDINATES: N42° 44.782' W91° 01.138'

7

⛺ Pinewoods Campground

Beauty ★★★★ / Privacy ★★★★ / Spaciousness ★★★ / Quiet ★★★★ / Security ★★★★ / Cleanliness ★★★★

The glacially altered landforms here offer many sights to see at Kettle Moraine South State Forest.

Everyone has heard that glaciers created many of Wisconsin's landforms. However, you will be hard-pressed to find someplace with so many glacial features in one area, as here at the South Unit of the Kettle Moraine State Forest. A forest visitor can see everything from the obvious kettle depressions and knobby hills to rare prairie marsh environments and spring-side wetlands called fens. Pinewoods Campground, located in the north end of the forest, makes for a quiet and attractive camp from which to explore these features.

Enter the campground and reach Loop 1. This loop is a 24-hour quiet zone, and no pets are allowed. Sites 6–36 are reservable. Campsites 16, 25, and 28 are walk-in sites. The last two require an uphill hike, but they are worth it for solitude. The beginning of Loop 1 is in a mix of field and forest. The loop then drops into white pinewoods after campsite 11. Thick underbrush screens campers from one another. Hilly terrain adds vertical variation to the widely separated sites.

Loop 2 houses sites 150–180. The first two sites, 150 and 151, are walk-in campsites. Drive a bit more and reach the rest of the loop. Heavy shade and thick woods of hickory-oak and other hardwoods characterize this site. Campsites 168–171 are somewhat open. The loop enters thick pinewoods after campsite 172.

Of the three loops, Loop 3 covers the most area, though it has only 36 campsites. This indicates how widespread sites 263–299 are. Pine trees loom over an understory that is dense, so dense in places that it diminishes the size of the campsite itself. Overall, these are great campsites. Campsites 270–299 are reservable. A large, modern shower building is available for all campers. Keep in mind that Pinewoods has a tendency to fill up on summer weekends.

There are many means by which to explore the forest: by foot, bike, watercraft, even horseback! Specific information on each option is available at the Ottawa Lake entrance station or the forest visitor center on WI 59 between Palmyra and Eagle. Dream a Horse Guided Trail Rides offers 1-hour rides through the forest. Call 608-403-1972 for

Access the Scuppernong Trail System from the campground. *photographed by Kevin Revolinski*

KEY INFORMATION

CONTACT: Wisconsin Department of Natural Resources, 262-594-6200, tinyurl.com/kmpinewoods; reservations 888-WI-PARKS, wisconsin.goingtocamp.com

OPEN: Mid-May–mid-October

SITES: 101

EACH SITE: Picnic table, fire grate

ASSIGNMENT: By phone; internet; or first come, first served

REGISTRATION: At Ottawa Lake Campground

FACILITIES: Hot showers, flush toilets, pit toilets, water spigots

PARKING: At campsites only

FEE: Wisconsin residents, $20; nonresidents, $25; $10 extra for electricity at wheelchair-accessible sites; plus vehicle admission fee (Wisconsin residents, $8; nonresidents, $11; Wisconsin residents age 65 and older, $3); $7.75 reservation fee

ELEVATION: 1,000'

RESTRICTIONS:

PETS: On leash only; prohibited in Loop 1

FIRES: In fire ring only; firewood must be purchased in state within 25 miles of campground

ALCOHOL: At campsites only

VEHICLES: 2/site

OTHER: 14-day stay limit; Loop 1 is a 24-hour quiet zone

reservations. More conventional means of travel include hiking, which can be done directly from the campground. A total of 54 miles of trails is available for hikers. Take the Green Trail south from the campground road to meet the Ice Age Trail, which travels 30 miles through the forest. The Green Trail is part of the Scuppernong Trail System that adds 12 miles of campground-accessible paths in addition to the Ice Age Trail. Of special interest is the nearby Scuppernong Springs Nature Trail, one of seven nature trails in the forest. This path explores the springs that have drawn people to the forest for centuries. Pass through Scuppernong Marsh, a restored wet prairie, and then past a marl works, where men extracted marl soil for fertilizer. An ancient campsite lies next to Indian Springs. Other springs here, such as Hotel Spring, offer stories of cultural history, available in a guidebook in the park office. Also in the historical vein are three frontier log cabins in the forest that have been restored and can be visited. Old World Wisconsin is a 576-acre rural museum run by the Wisconsin Historical Society. It has more than 60 old structures and other features. Old World Wisconsin is located south of Pinewoods on WI 67.

Road bikers will be pedaling the country lanes that run through and around the forest. The Emma Carlin and John Muir trail systems are available for hikers and bikers. Drivers will want to tour the lower half of the Kettle Moraine Scenic Drive that passes directly by Pinewoods Campground.

On hot days, campers will be heading to Ottawa Lake, a kettle lake formed when a huge chunk of ice slowly melted, creating a depression that filled with water. A swim beach lies along this body of water. This "no gas motors" lake is also an angling destination. Paddlers can follow the self-guided canoe trail to learn more about Ottawa Lake and its relationship to the time of glaciers. No matter your mode of transportation, the South Unit of Kettle Moraine State Forest makes for an interesting destination, especially with a campground as nice as Pinewoods.

Pinewoods Campground

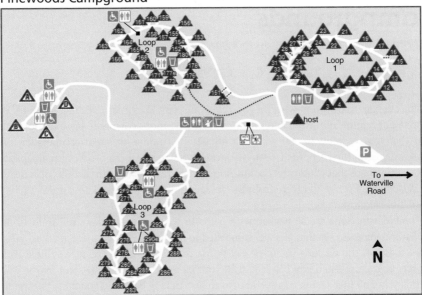

GETTING THERE

From Exit 282 on I-94, take WI 67 south 9 miles to Ottawa Lake Campground. You must register here. From Ottawa Lake, take WI 67 south 0.4 mile to County Road ZZ. Turn left on CR ZZ and follow it 1.6 miles to Waterville Road. Turn left on Waterville Road and follow it 1.2 miles to Pinewoods Campground on your left.

GPS COORDINATES: N42° 56.975' W88° 26.523'

8

⛺ Sidie Hollow County Park Campgrounds

Beauty ★★★ / Privacy ★★★ / Spaciousness ★★★ / Quiet ★★★★★ / Security ★★★ / Cleanliness ★★★★

Sidie Hollow is a great "get away from it all" destination.

Do you ever get to the point where if you get in one more traffic jam, see one more TV commercial, get one more unsolicited email, or hear one more coworker say one more stupid thing that you are going to tear your hair out? Then it's time for a tent-camping trip. Time to get away from the rush, rush, rush madness of our modern era. And I have the place for you—somewhere that exudes relaxation, somewhere tucked away in the hills of southwestern Wisconsin. Even if you were from the area, you might not even know it was there. It is called Sidie Hollow.

Some destinations are so packed with paths to walk, rivers to float, rail-trails to pedal, and natural things to see that you feel compelled to do them. This "go there, do that" pressure sometimes kills the relaxing intent of a camping trip. There is no pressure at Sidie Hollow. It is scenic for sure—and you can fish, float your canoe around the lake, and maybe walk in the valley, but all that seems an afterthought to just kicking back and watching the sun move across the sky. Or maybe taking a nap in the lounge chair. This slow-paced Vernon County park outside the town of Viroqua is so relaxed that they give turtles speeding tickets!

Set on the shores of Sidie Hollow Lake, an impound of a feeder branch of the South Fork of the Bad Axe River, this campground has three distinct sections. Tall, forested hills

Peaceful Sidie Hollow Lake

photographed by Jen AnneTastic

KEY INFORMATION

CONTACT: Vernon County Parks, 608-637-5480, tinyurl.com/sidiehollowpark

OPEN: April 15–October 15

SITES: 35 primitive, 21 electric, 17 full hookups

EACH SITE: Picnic table, fire grate

ASSIGNMENT: By phone; internet; or first come, first served

REGISTRATION: At camp office

FACILITIES: Hot showers, flush toilets, vault toilets, water spigots, playground, boat access

PARKING: At campsites only

FEE: $15 ($21 electric site)

ELEVATION: 675'

RESTRICTIONS:

PETS: On leash only

FIRES: In fire ring only

ALCOHOL: At campsites only

VEHICLES: No restrictions

OTHER: Quiet hours 11 p.m.–7 a.m.

add a remote touch to the setting. Coming from Viroqua, leave County Road XX and turn left to reach the first section, at the head of the lake. Sites 1–3 are set beneath tall trees beside a wooded stream, Sidie Hollow Creek. These are the best sites in this hollow and are great for tent campers. The next 12 sites are along a dead-end road and have electricity. The sites away from the creek are sun-baked. A playground, picnic shelter, water spigot, and vault toilet serve this area better suited for big rigs. The boat launch for this "no gas motors" lake lies near this area. Showers and flush toilets are nearby.

The second area lies 0.8 mile farther down County Road XX. This is the largest camping area. A small, clear trout stream forms the hollow. The first sites are banked against hardwood trees by the stream and have a grassy understory. Some sites may get too much sun, but all are well spaced from one another. The campground stretches down the hollow, with sites on both sides of the road. Wooded hills give the clean campground an intimate feel. A mix of trees shades the grassy tent sites. One section near the office has electrical sites favored by larger rigs. Here is where you'll also find showers and flush toilets.

Pass the campground office and come to a picnic shelter with a nice lake view. To the left of the shelter are four good tent sites that require a short walk from the parking area. Surprisingly, these sites are lesser used, though the campground as a whole has a lightly used look. Water spigots and vault toilets are set in this hollow.

The third area rests on a ridgetop. The left turn, Camp Site Road, is 4 miles after getting on CR XX. This heavily wooded hilltop camp is much less used than the others. I will personally guarantee that this third camp never fills! The 20 shaded sites lie on either side of the road. They are literally cut into a hickory, cherry, oak, and aspen forest and are ideal for the solitude seeker. This area is a getaway from the "get away from it all" destination that is Sidie Hollow. A water spigot and vault toilets are located up here too.

Trails leave every camping area and connect to a master path circling Sidie Hollow Lake. You can use this path for bank fishing or merely to stretch your legs. Anglers try their luck for panfish and trout in Sidie Hollow Lake. Others will fish the small creeks feeding Sidie Hollow Lake. Supplies can be had in nearby Viroqua. My advice to you is to get everything you need, set up camp, and go into relaxation mode. We could all use more of that.

Sidie Hollow County Park: Main Campground

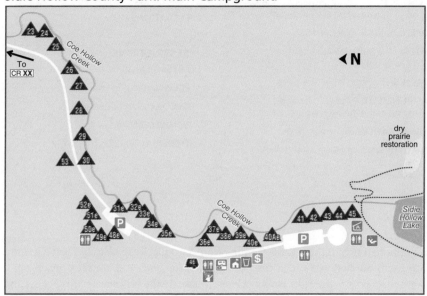

Sidie Hollow County Park: Boat Landing Campground

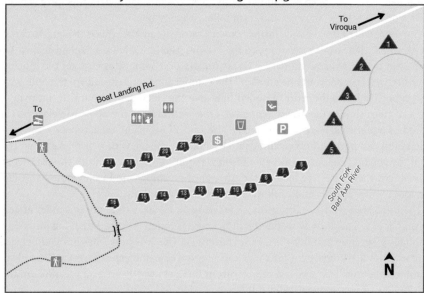

Sidie Hollow County Park: Upper Campground

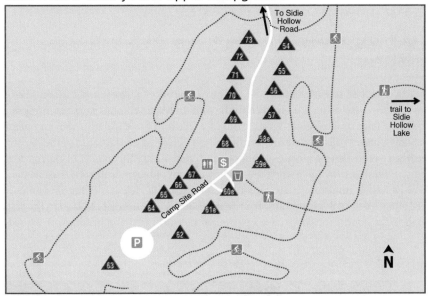

GETTING THERE

From downtown Viroqua, take WI 56 west 1.7 miles to County Road XX. Turn left on CR XX and follow it 2 miles to a left turn to the first camp area, 2.8 miles to the second camp area, and 4 miles to the third camp area. All are marked with signs.

GPS COORDINATES: N43° 32.719' W90° 57.624'

9

Tower Hill State Park Campground

Beauty ★★★★ / Privacy ★★★ / Spaciousness ★★★ / Quiet ★★★ / Security ★★ / Cleanliness ★★★★

This small and quiet campground lies along the banks of the Lower Wisconsin State Riverway.

How Tower Hill State Park came to be is a mix of location, history, and chance. Lead was discovered in southwestern Wisconsin in the mid-1820s. Sometime later, an entrepreneur from Green Bay named Daniel Whitney hired a fellow to build a shot tower, an operation for making musket balls from lead, near the village of Helena on the banks of the Wisconsin River. The river made transporting the shot quite convenient. The hamlet of Helena grew as a result of the shot tower, but when the tower went out of business in 1864, Helena died. In 1889, a Unitarian minister, Jenkin Lloyd Jones, bought the Helena site for $60. Jones built some cottages before dying in 1918. Four years later, his wife deeded the land to the state of Wisconsin for a park. Today, we have a preserved slice of beauty and history with a good but

The hiking trail to the shot tower passes beneath carved sandstone.

KEY INFORMATION

CONTACT: Wisconsin Department of Natural Resources, 608-935-2315, tinyurl.com/TowerHillSP; reservations 888-WI-PARKS, wisconsin.goingtocamp.com

OPEN: May–October

SITES: 11

EACH SITE: Picnic table, fire ring, wood bench

ASSIGNMENT: By phone, internet, or first come, first served

REGISTRATION: At park office

FACILITIES: Vault toilet, water spigot

PARKING: At campsites only

FEE: Wisconsin residents: $16; nonresidents:

$21; plus vehicle admission fee (Wisconsin resident, $8; nonresidents, $11; Wisconsin resident age 65 and older, $3); $7.75 reservation fee

ELEVATION: 450'

RESTRICTIONS:

PETS: On leash only

FIRES: In fire ring only; firewood must be purchased in state within 25 miles of campground

ALCOHOL: At campsites only

VEHICLES: 2/site

OTHER: 14-day stay limit

---

small campground. You can visit the shot tower, canoe the Lower Wisconsin State River-way, and enjoy some other nearby attractions.

Due to budget cuts this park is often without a ranger, and, in fact, calling the park number will likely connect you to someone at Governor Dodge State Park. In this case you must self-register. For such a small campground, Tower Hill has vastly different sites. Pass the park office and the remains of a stone barn. The first two campsites lie to the left on an access road to Mill Creek, which immediately flows into the Wisconsin River. The first site on the left is mostly grassy and receives afternoon shade from a line of trees. Four sites have been closed over the years, giving a bit more privacy to site 1 and leaving the best of the bunch, site 3, all alone down on the banks of Mill Creek, offering maximum privacy. A canoe landing lies at the end of this road. A canoe rack is available for campers by the water.

The next group of sites is set along a loop road. A grassy picnic area shaded by trees occupies the middle of the loop. While sites 2, 4, 5, and 6 no longer exist, the remaining sites have not been renumbered. Between the loop and Mill Creek stand two nice sites on a level flat shaded by pines. The next site, 9, is all alone in a grassy area divided by trees. Two vault toilets are across the road from 10, which offers pine needles for a tent spot. Grassy campsite 11 offers a stone fireplace and is also shaded with trees. This was my choice. Campsites 12 and 13 are a bit open in a grassy area. Campsite 14 lies beneath a majestic white pine, but the ground here is a bit sloped. Campsite 15 has been leveled and is a well-shaded walk-up site.

Start your Tower Hill adventure with a visit to the shot tower. Imagine this park through its various transformations as you take the short trail to the tower. Next, you may want to canoe the Lower Wisconsin State Riverway. From nearby Sauk City, the last 93 miles of this connector to the Mississippi River are undammed and offer surprisingly natural scenery, as land continues to be purchased along the waterway. The 10-mile canoe run from Arena to nearby Spring Green is popular. The farther you go down the river, the more remote your experience. Several canoe liveries make trips easy, even if you don't have your own canoe. Use their shuttles if you have your own boat. A list of liveries is available at the park office.

Both Mill Creek and the Wisconsin River have great fishing at normal water levels. Mill Creek can be fished for trout by foot. Return to WI 18 and turn left, then left again on County Road T, and look for the signs indicating the public fishing areas. A hot day will find careful swimmers at Peterson Landing on the Wisconsin River, across the WI 18 bridge toward Spring Green. Watch out for the river, though; it can flow deceptively fast.

Just down the road from Tower Hill is an array of attractions from sophisticated to hokey. The House on the Rock is an unusual house that has transformed into a display of anything out of the ordinary, from the world's largest carousel to a miniature circus. The Frank Lloyd Wright Visitor Center and his nearby Taliesin house give insight into the architectural genius. Wright described the house and its furnishings as his autobiography. The American Players Theatre offers outdoor (and some indoor) Shakespearean and other plays. Just north of Tower Hill is the town of Spring Green, which has turned into a cultural mecca from the influence of the Frank Lloyd Wright house. I can't help but wonder what this whole area would be like today if the shot tower hadn't been built on the banks of the Wisconsin River at the confluence of Mill Creek.

Tower Hill State Park Campground

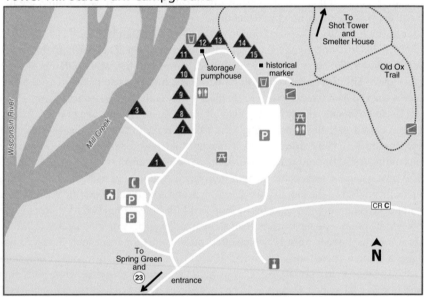

GETTING THERE

From Spring Green, head south on WI 23, crossing the Wisconsin River after 2 miles. Turn left on County Road C and follow it 1 mile to the park, on your left.

GPS COORDINATES: N43° 08.863' W90° 02.873'

10

⚠ Wildcat Mountain State Park Campground

Beauty ★★★ / Privacy ★★★ / Spaciousness ★★★★ / Quiet ★★★★ / Security ★★★ / Cleanliness ★★★★★

Wildcat Mountain is an active camper's destination.

The campground at this state park is really on top of a mountain. The view from the observation area will attest to that. Furthermore, the lack of water up top makes it one of the least buggy campgrounds in the state. Remember that when you are enjoying the mountain breezes in your folding chair while others are pouring on the bug dope and diving headlong into their tents. However, odds are that you will be engaging in the many activities here—hiking the steep and challenging trails, canoeing the famed Kickapoo River, or bicycling some of Wisconsin's most famous rail-trails.

Enter the campground after chugging uphill from Ontario. You'll pass the entrance station, which in 2011 eliminated sites 17–21. The drive-up sites start beyond here with 22–27 in a grassy flat broken by white pines, sugar maples, and other planted trees. Most of the sites are on a level, grassy slope. What they lack in privacy, they make up for in spaciousness. The planted trees are far enough along to provide shade for most any tent. Campers drive onto the grassy area to park.

The main road then ends. Turn right and pass 4 more sites that are even larger than the previous 10 sites. The campground host occupies one of these sites. Reach the modern bathhouse with hot showers and water spigots. The loop portion of the campground offers

Canoeing the Kickapoo River   *photographed by Kevin Revolinski*

KEY INFORMATION

CONTACT: Wisconsin Department of Natural Resources, 608-337-4775, tinyurl.com /WildcatMtn; reservations 888-WI-PARKS, wisconsin.goingtocamp.com

OPEN: Year-round; water and bathhouse open May–October, but only 4 sites plowed in winter

SITES: 25 primitive, 20 walk-in

EACH SITE: Picnic table, fire ring

ASSIGNMENT: By phone; internet; or first come, first served

REGISTRATION: At entrance station

FACILITIES: Hot showers, flush toilets, pit toilets, water spigots, carts for toting gear to campsites

PARKING: At campsites only

FEE: Wisconsin residents, $20 ($30 electric site); nonresidents, $25 ($35 electric site); plus vehicle admission fee (Wisconsin residents, $8; nonresidents, $11; Wisconsin residents age 65 and older, $3); $7.75 reservation fee

PARKING: At campsites only

ELEVATION: 1,265'

RESTRICTIONS:

PETS: On leash only

FIRES: In fire ring only; firewood must be purchased in state within 25 miles of campground

ALCOHOL: At campsites only

VEHICLES: 2/site

OTHER: 14-day stay limit

---

an entirely different setting. Sites 1–13 are perched on the cusp of Wildcat Mountain. Trees mostly block views, but the land dropping off from the campsites has a mountain atmosphere. The sites on the inside of the loop are more open, but the sites on the outside of the loop are mostly shaded and some of the campground's best. Campsite 1 is all alone. Pass a vault toilet for either sex. Reservation makers coming in blind should consider sites 6, 7, 9, and 11. Pass a set of vault toilets, and then reach a miniloop (sites 13–16) with a road so narrow that no big rig would dare drive in. Campsite 14 has a mountain view through the trees. Campsite 16 is on the inside of this miniloop and is the only site in the park that I do not recommend.

But the really golden choices are the cart-in sites. These offer more privacy and no vehicle traffic. They lie to the west of the drive-up loop and are laid out in a large loop (101–115) and a smaller half loop (116–120) located just north of the bathhouse. Use one of the park's provided carts to haul your gear into the woods from parking areas either next to the entrance station or near the bathhouse. A gravel trail connects the sites, all of which have mowed grass and plenty of shade. Sites 104 and the nearly conjoined 106 and 107 are a bit more open than the others. Site 119 has a long hooking trail to get off the gravel path and thus has become the park favorite. All of these are reservable, and you may need to plan far in advance to nab them in summer. Wildcat Mountain will fill on nice summer weekends, so I encourage visitors to make reservations when they decide to come. Overflow can consider the 24 electric sites at the horse camp if they don't mind the trailers.

This place will make you rethink just how appealing this area of the state can be if you didn't already know. The primary draw is the Kickapoo River. A canoe landing is down the mountain in the state park. Several liveries in nearby Ontario make renting a canoe or getting a shuttle easy. The park office has a list of operators. The water is swift enough to make the float fun but doable by most everyone, and the waterway makes unending twists and turns among sandstone cliffs and thick woods.

The hiking trails here will test you. The Hemlock Trail cruises along the Kickapoo River and enters old-growth woods before switchbacking up to the top of Mount Pisgah and a great vista. It then drops steeply to the water again. The Old Settlers Trail starts near Observation Point (a must) and goes up and down through hardwood forests and pinewoods and past small creeks and rock formations. The Ice Cave Trail provides a short walk to the mouth of a rock overhang, where a spring makes ice formations in winter. Bicyclers have already heard of the Elroy–Sparta State Trail. This 32-mile rail-trail was one of the nation's first. It passes through three tunnels on the way, the longest being 3,810 feet long! Bring your flashlight. The 400 State Trail travels 22 miles between Elroy and Reedsburg, passing small villages along the way. The La Crosse River Trail extends 21 miles across the La Crosse River Valley. The park office and state park websites are full of information about these rail-trails.

And if that isn't enough to keep you busy, fish Billings Creek, a great trout stream on Wildcat Mountain and Kickapoo Valley Reserve property. It has some fine brown trout. The Kickapoo Valley Reserve is 8,500 acres of state-owned wilderness adjacent to Wildcat. Hiking and mountain biking trails await in this lower portion of the Kickapoo River Valley. Tributaries of the Kickapoo provide more angling opportunities. Grab a reserve map at the Wildcat park office or visit kvr.state.wi.us for more information on Kickapoo Valley Reserve, and then head for Wildcat Mountain.

Wildcat Mountain State Park Campground

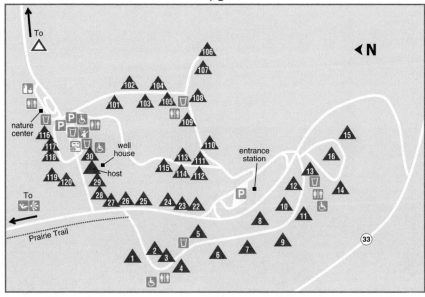

GETTING THERE

From Ontario, take WI 33 2 miles south to the park, on your left.

GPS COORDINATES: N43° 42.145' W90° 34.753'

11

Wyalusing State Park Campgrounds

Beauty ★★★★★ / Privacy ★★★ / Spaciousness ★★★★ / Quiet ★★★ / Securit: ★★★★★ / Cleanliness ★★★★

Choosing between the two excellent campgrounds is only the first of several win–win decisions here.

Wondering why Wyalusing was among the first candidates for a state park in Wisconsin? Was it the aboriginal mounds, settler history, or the incredible views of the Mississippi River–Wisconsin River confluence? No matter the actual reason, the reasoning was sound. Wisconsinites should be proud of this trail-laced jewel with two good yet different campgrounds.

Homestead Campground and Wisconsin Ridge Campground offer distinctly different reasons to pitch a tent. The views from Wisconsin Ridge will astound you. Enter a long, narrow loop with a fine bathhouse. The first few sites on the outside of the loop have no view but are heavily shaded with hardwoods and would make a fine tenter's camp. A steep hill drops sharply away from the camps. The inside loop sites have limited views and no privacy. The

From the scenic overlook, you can see where the Wisconsin River meets the Mississippi.

photographed by Kevin Revolinski

KEY INFORMATION

CONTACT: Wisconsin Department of Natural Resources, 608-996-2261, tinyurl.com /wyalusingSP; reservations 888-WI-PARKS, wisconsin.goingtocamp.com

OPEN: Wisconsin Ridge, year-round; Homestead, May–October

SITES: 76 primitive, 33 electric

EACH SITE: Picnic table, fire ring

ASSIGNMENT: By phone; internet; or first come, first served

REGISTRATION: At visitor center

FACILITIES: Hot showers, flush toilets, pit toilets, water spigots

PARKING: At campsites only

FEE: Wisconsin residents, $18 ($30 electric site); nonresidents, $23 ($35 electric site); plus vehicle admission fee (Wisconsin residents, $8; nonresidents, $11; Wisconsin residents age 65 and older, $3); $7.75 reservation fee

ELEVATION: 1,100'

RESTRICTIONS:

PETS: On leash only

FIRES: In fire ring only; firewood must be purchased in state within 25 miles of campground

ALCOHOL: At campsites only

VEHICLES: 2/site

OTHER: 14-day stay limit

---

loop curves past the Knob Picnic Shelter, one of many attractive stone structures built by the Civilian Conservation Corps. The sites with views start with 119. And they are million-dollar views. The last 14 sites on this loop are first come, first served. If you reserve a site here, make sure to ask if it is on the outside of the loop with a number higher than 118.

A price is paid for this view. The sites with a view are small and have no privacy. Some have limited shade. But it seems that campers are nearly always looking out to the vastness below and beyond. The other downside: this campground and Homestead Campground are sure to fill during high summer weekends. Consider coming some early fall weekend or during the week anytime.

What Homestead Campground lacks in views, it makes up for in being an all-around great place to camp, with its large, grassy campsites well spaced from one another and broken with thick brush for maximum privacy. Four spur roads with miniloops emanate from a larger center loop. The center loop has a bathhouse, water spigot, and pit toilet. The first spur, with sites 201–219, offers a mix of sunny and shaded sites beneath pine, oak, sumac, and cherry trees. Site 211 offers excellent shade and solitude. The second spur is smaller and on a hill. Site 225 also has good shade and solitude. The third spur, with sites 229–244, has heavy brush for privacy but limited shade. The sites at the end of the spur are first come, first served in deep dark woods. The final spur, with sites 245–255, has some sunny and some shaded sites. The Turkey Hollow Trail leaves from the back of this spur.

The Turkey Hollow Trail is but a portion of 22 total miles of feature-packed paths at Wyalusing. All the trails are interconnected, so you can start hiking directly from either campground. Want to see some of the American Indian mounds? Take the Sentinel Ridge Trail, which circles some mounds on the way down to the Mississippi River and gives added historical information about the mound builders, voyageurs, Black Robes, and others who passed this way. The Bluff Trail passes Treasure Cave, Signal Point, and Point Lookout, where you are sure to get an eyeful. Check out a waterfall and Pictured Rock Cave on the

Sugar Maple Nature Trail. Sand Cave Trail also has a waterfall. Pass through the Keyhole on the Bluff Trail.

The above is just a sampling of the trails. Some paths are open to bicycles, too, so check the comprehensive park trails map. If you don't feel like hiking, how about a canoe trip? A signed 6-mile canoe trail circles through sloughs on the Mississippi and then down the mighty river itself. Many watery wildflowers bloom during summer. A concessionaire rents canoes and kayaks from the nature center, located near Wisconsin Ridge Campground.

Wyalusing is popular with many bird-watchers. They invade the campgrounds late April–mid-May. More species of birds can be seen here than any other park in the state. A full-time naturalist leads programs about birds and much more. Call ahead for exact programs and schedules. Anglers will be scouring the backwaters of the Mississippi and Wisconsin Rivers for panfish, bass, northern pike, and walleye. A fishing pier is located at the park's boat landing. Hot days will find campers driving 2 miles south to Wyalusing Recreation Area, a Grant County park that has a swim beach and boat landing on the Mississippi River. Finally, a group called the Starsplitters has installed observatories at the state park. They will be glad to introduce you to astronomy—only at night, though. With all the things to do at Wyalusing, choosing your campground doesn't seem quite as difficult.

Wyalusing State Park: Homestead Campground

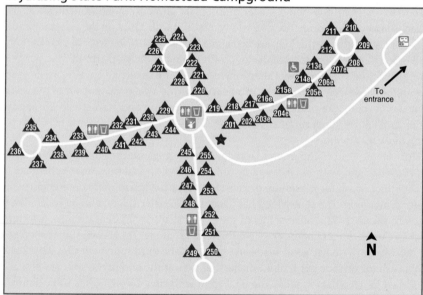

Wyalusing State Park: Wisconsin Ridge Campground

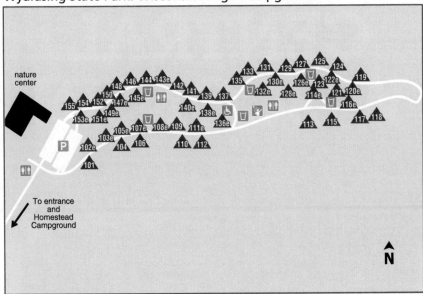

GETTING THERE

From Prairie du Chien, head east on US 18 for 7 miles to cross the Wisconsin River. Turn right on County Road C and follow it 3 miles to CR X. Turn right on CR X and follow it 1 mile to the state park, on your right.

GPS COORDINATES: N42° 59.632' W91° 06.955'

CENTRAL WISCONSIN

Dells of the Eau Claire (see page 52)

photographed by Mandy Kersten Hayungs

12

Buckhorn State Park Campground

Beauty ★★★★★ / Privacy ★★★★ / Spaciousness ★★★★★ / Quiet ★★★ / Security ★★★★ / Cleanliness ★★★★

Most of the camps here are lakeside walk-in sites.

Buckhorn is an evolving park in a wild area that keeps improving over time. For starters, it has backpack campsites. I call them extended walk-in sites. These walk-in sites range from less than 100 feet from car to campsite to more than a mile to the camp. However, don't mark this park off your list because you don't have a backpack; Buckhorn provides carts to carry your gear from the parking area to the campsite (you still have to walk, though). There is also another option. Because these sites are on the shores of Castle Rock Lake, you can "boat-in" your gear! If you are still not convinced that this park is for you, Buckhorn does have 59 conventional drive-up campsites in a long double loop in the northwest corner of the park (8 of them have electricity). Wherever you choose to camp, you can enjoy the wilderness surrounding Wisconsin's fourth-largest lake.

The sites at Buckhorn are located in several clusters spread throughout the peninsula-shaped park. Campsites are numbered but do not follow any numerical order outside of the clusters themselves. Starting in the northeast section and going around the peninsula in a clockwise fashion, the first cluster includes sites 1–3, located just off 22nd Avenue, a 300-yard walk from a dedicated parking lot. The name belies the gravel road's true rustic nature. These sites are mostly wooded and share a small sandy beach ideal for kids. About 0.7 mile south and 100 yards from parking is the second cluster. Also located just off 22nd Avenue, campsites 20–22 have lake access. These are more desirable than 30–33, which lack the water access and lie within 22nd Avenue and 33rd Street. Sites 39–42 are south from there, across 33rd Street and a 40-yard walk in.

The group camp offers 11 sites total, but B1–B3 are truly for larger groups. Families nevertheless use sites A1–A8, which are mostly shaded and have intervening trees and brush but are not as private as the other walk-in sites. There are two clusters between the group camp and the lake. Sites 43–45 are a 350-yard hike in, while 34–37 shave 50 yards off that trek. The next cluster encountered is

The shoreline of Castle Rock Lake as seen from campsite 4

photographed by Jen AnneTastic

CONTACT: Wisconsin Department of Natural Resources, 608-565-2789, tinyurl.com /buckhornSP; reservations 888-WI-PARKS, wisconsin.goingtocamp.com

OPEN: May–October; 3 sites open year-round

SITES: 105 primitive, 10 electric

EACH SITE: Picnic table, fire grate, lantern post, wood bench

ASSIGNMENT: By phone; internet; or first come, first served

REGISTRATION: At park office or self-registration if office is closed

FACILITIES: Hot showers, flush toilets, pump well, vault toilet, carts for toting gear to campsites

PARKING: At campsites and walk-in site parking

FEE: Wisconsin residents, $18; nonresidents, $28; plus vehicle admission fee (Wisconsin residents, $8; nonresidents, $11; Wisconsin residents age 65 and older, $3); $7.75 reservation fee

ELEVATION: 885′

RESTRICTIONS:

PETS: On leash only

FIRES: In fire ring only; firewood must be purchased in state within 25 miles of campground

ALCOHOL: At campsites only

VEHICLES: 2/site

OTHER: 14-day stay limit

located on the southwest side of the peninsula—sites 4–7, 13–15, and 17–19. Campsites 4–7 sit on a small peninsula overlooking the lake and require a 0.7-mile walk, but they are worth the effort. Of special note is site 6, located on a lakefront point beneath a stand of white pines. Campsite 7 is for solitude lovers. Campsites 13–15 are set in heavier woods along the shore and require a 0.4-mile walk. Campsites 17–19 are the farthest—1.25 miles— and are often reached by boat.

Continuing north around the peninsula, you'll find the fourth cluster: 8–12, 16, and 23–25. Campsites 8, 9, and 16 have a very short walk—8 even has electricity and a paved path to the site for disabled campers. Campsites 10–12 and 25 are set on an open peninsula after a 200-yard walk. Shade is scarce here, but a small wood shelter keeps campers out of the elements. Campsites 23–24 share a lightly wooded point with a great lake view. The final cluster includes campsites 26–29, which share a parking lot and are strung out along a trail that leads to the conventional campsites. The walk in ranges from 30 to 155 yards, with 26 being the farthest. All are partly shaded by river birch trees.

Each campsite cluster has a portable toilet within an easy walk. Water can be had at the main backpack parking area and park office. Cold showers can be had at the south beach park, and hot showers and flush toilets are located just south of the amphitheater near the south parking lot. Be advised that late spring and early summer can be buggy at Buckhorn. Call ahead for the latest mosquito report. Bugs or not, these sites will fill on summer weekends. No wonder—these are some of the best tent campsites in the state. The lakeside setting is simply beautiful. Most campers set up and enjoy the park from their little havens. Fishing and boating are just steps away. Castle Rock Flowage, as this dammed reservoir on the Wisconsin River is also known, is famous for its walleye fishing. But that is only the beginning. Try your luck with bass (largemouth and smallmouth), plus toothy pike and panfish. Bank-fish from your campsite or use the pier at the North Picnic Area. Whether you are on your feet or in a motorboat or canoe, the angling is quite scenic here.

Canoeists have an additional venue to stroke their paddle—the Canoe Interpretive Trail. This marked route plies one of the many sloughs that make up the park. And if you don't have a canoe or kayak, the park will be glad to rent you one at the start of the paddle trail. It will also loan you a fishing rod free of charge. If you are into games, borrow a volleyball for use at the court near the 300-foot-long swim beach, or borrow some horseshoes. If you are interested in geocaching, stop in at the park office and borrow one of their GPS units preloaded with geocaches both here and at Roche-A-Cri State Park (see page 79).

Campers will quickly learn the trails here—they are used to access the campsites. I walked them all on my visit. Learn about the sands of the central part of the state on the Nature Trail. Traverse wetlands on wood bridges. A hiker is just about guaranteed to see deer and turkeys here. Check out the short Sandblow Walk. Just don't let the lack of a backpack keep you from tent camping at Buckhorn.

Buckhorn State Park Campground

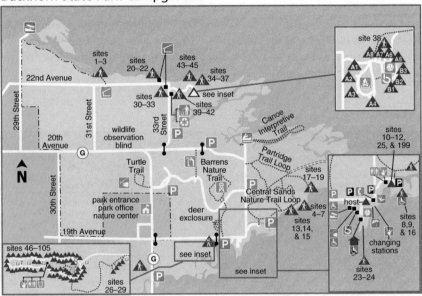

GETTING THERE

From Exit 61 on I-90/94, take WI 80 north 7 miles to WI 58. Turn right on WI 58 and follow it 3 miles to County Road G. Turn left on CR G and follow it 3 miles to Buckhorn, on your right.

GPS COORDINATES: N43° 56.770' W89° 59.745'

13

Dells of the Eau Claire County Park Campground

Beauty ★★★ / Privacy ★★★ / Spaciousness ★★★ / Quiet ★★★ / Security ★★★★ / Cleanliness ★★★★★

These dells deserve their designation as a state natural area.

All Wisconsinites should see the Dells of the Eau Claire. After all, the state deemed them significant enough to be preserved as a state natural area. The park's name might confuse folks trying to locate it. These are not the Dells that are so well known in Wisconsin; those Dells are located on the Wisconsin River and are surrounded by tourist traps. No, the Dells of the Eau Claire are located on the Eau Claire River, just east of Wausau in Marathon County, which operates the campground, trails, and swim beach. The name Eau Claire can also add to the confusion—Wisconsin has an Eau Claire County, the city of Eau Claire, and three Eau Claire Rivers. Regardless of the confusion, visiting this park is well worth your time. Visitors will see amazing rock formations surrounded by cascading water and unusual plants. This recreational development has enhanced the work of Mother Nature, making these dells easier for tent campers to enjoy.

Rock formations of the Dells

photographed by Mandy Kersten Hayungs

KEY INFORMATION

CONTACT: Marathon County, 715-261-1550, tinyurl.com/dellseauclaire; reservations online, or 715-261-1566, 9 a.m.–3 p.m.

OPEN: May–October

SITES: 12 primitive, 16 electric

EACH SITE: Picnic table, fire grate

ASSIGNMENT: By phone, internet or first come, first served

REGISTRATION: Park manager will come by and register you; self-registration Labor Day–Memorial Day

FACILITIES: Vault toilets, pump well

PARKING: At campsites only

FEE: $15 ($18 electric site); $7 reservation fee

ELEVATION: 1,300'

RESTRICTIONS:

PETS: On leash only

FIRES: In fire ring only

ALCOHOL: At campsites only

VEHICLES: 2/site

OTHER: 14-day stay limit

I don't want to mislead you—the natural landscape is the star of the show here. It was 2 million years in the making. The campground works, but it is no destination unto itself. It—like the rest of the park—is well kept, neat, and in good shape. Enter the campground, which is laid out in a loop. Pass the telephone, pump well, and vault toilets. The first 16 sites are equipped with electricity and are reservable, except for site 2. These smallish sites may contain pop-ups, but not a whole lot of big rigs will fit in. The first few sites on the inside of the loop are surrounded by forest but are open overhead, where a telephone line cuts through the campground. The good sites begin with 8. If you want to reserve a site, go with 8, 9, or 10.

The loop curves around, and the sites become shaded and private. Grass and/or sand covers the campsite floors. These sites are also reservable, except for sites 18, 20, 22, and 24. The sites on this loop are as good and generally better than the first 16 sites, though only 27 and 28 have electricity. However, this campground fills on holidays and nice summer weekends. The park manager lives on the premises during the camping season, enhancing campsite security, which can be questionable at some county parks.

Like much of the Wisconsin landscape, the dells themselves are of glacial origin. The frothy waters of the Eau Claire crash, twist, and work their way among broken boulders, outcrops, crags, and steplike platforms, forming waterfalls and cascades. Visitors hopping from rock to rock near the river will also notice "potholes," smooth depressions carved into the rock back when the glaciers were melting. Rock-hopping isn't the only thing you can do on your feet here. A network of interconnected trails has been laid out in this geologically significant valley. The High Bridge downstream from the Dells of the Eau Claire enables hikers to make a loop through rich fern woods along both sides of the river. The forest's dark "fairyland" nature contrasts with rocky dells open to the sky overhead. The high ground is covered in pine. Even a short section of the Ice Age Trail passes through the Dells of the Eau Claire. The entire trail network can be accessed directly from the campground.

One trail leads from the campground to the picnic area/swim beach on the banks of the Eau Claire River above the dells. A grassy lawn with both sun and shade stands above steps leading down to the beach. Changing rooms are conveniently close. The park urges campers to dip at the swim beach and not take their chances in the swiftly moving waters near the dells.

Another picnic area features a large playground for kids near some rustic-looking open-sided shelters. As you look around, you will agree that this park is so well maintained that Marathon County should receive kudos. Remember, the natural scenery here outstrips any shortcomings the campground may have. So put the Dells of the Eau Claire on your must-do list of natural Wisconsin, now that you know where they are.

Dells of the Eau Claire County Park Campground

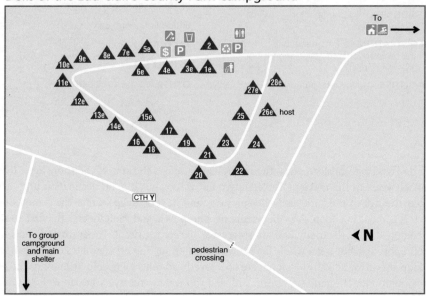

GETTING THERE

From downtown Wausau, take Franklin Street east, and stay with it as it becomes County Road Z. Follow Franklin Street/CR Z 14.5 miles to County Trunk Highway Y. Turn left on CTH Y and follow it 1.7 miles to the park.

GPS COORDINATES: N45° 00.335' W89° 20.270'

14

East Fork Campground

Beauty ★★★★★ / Privacy ★★★★ / Spaciousness ★★★★★ / Quiet ★★★★ / Security ★★★ / Cleanliness ★★★★

East Fork is your base camp for exploring the north side of the Black River State Forest.

The timber wolf has returned to the forests of the Black River in Jackson County. So should you, especially with a campground as nice as East Fork, set on the banks of East Fork Black River. From here, you can explore some 67,000 acres of the Black River State Forest, which offers everything from excellent canoeing and fishing to hiking and wildlife-watching.

The timber wolf was extirpated from Wisconsin in the late 1950s, about when Black River State Forest was established. Since then, things have really looked up for both the timber wolf and the state forest. The wolves have returned. From your campsite on the East Fork Black River, you may even hear the call of a pack of wolves roaming.

Reach the convenient campground canoe ramp at the end of Campground Road, and then turn into the campground, which lies along a road paralleling the beautiful East Fork

Banks of the East Fork Black River

KEY INFORMATION

CONTACT: Wisconsin Department of Natural Resources, 715-284-4103, dnr.wi.gov /topic/StateForests/blackriver; reservations 888-WI-PARKS, wisconsin.goingtocamp.com

OPEN: Mid-April–mid-October

SITES: 24

EACH SITE: Picnic table, fire grate

ASSIGNMENT: By phone and internet May 1 to mid-October or first come, first served

REGISTRATION: Self-registration on-site or at entrance station

FACILITIES: Vault toilets, pump well

PARKING: At campsites only

FEE: Wisconsin residents, $16; nonresidents, $26; plus vehicle admission fee (Wisconsin residents, $8; nonresidents, $11; Wisconsin residents age 65 and older, $3); $7.75 reservation fee

ELEVATION: 900'

RESTRICTIONS:

PETS: On leash only

FIRES: In fire ring only; firewood must be purchased in state within 25 miles of campground

ALCOHOL: At campsites only

VEHICLES: 2/site

OTHER: Use of generators prohibited

to your left and a marsh to your right. Pass a vault toilet for each gender and a firewood shed. A mix of sugar maple, red pine, white pine, oak, and scattered birch trees shade the campground. Younger trees, brush, and ferns galore provide privacy. The sites themselves are sand and mown grass. Pass by a pump well; another pump well is located about 0.25 mile back on Campground Road.

Most of the sites on the left side of the road offer river views and river access, at least enough to grab a view or toss in a line. The sites away from the river are less used and offer more privacy. But don't get the idea that this is a used and abused campground—no way. It is clean, well kept, and naturally beautiful. A miniloop at the end of the road has three sites, of which the most private is 22. A short nature trail departs up the East Fork from the end of the loop.

This is a first-come, first-served campground, and you will almost certainly be served—even someone arriving late Friday on a holiday weekend will most likely get a site. I was the only person there during my weekday visit. But, just like the timber wolf, once you come here, you will return. The timber wolf returned to Wisconsin around the late 1980s, a result of timber wolf protection in neighboring Minnesota during the early 1970s, which led to offspring expanding their range. The first wolves were spotted in the Black River State Forest in 1994. Don't expect to see one, but just knowing that they are there gives a little extra verve to the forest.

You can expect to enjoy canoeing the East Fork Black River with its mild rapids. The stream has good fishing for bass and walleye. A popular excursion starts from Pray Road and meanders to the campground landing—a trip of about 10 miles. Shorter runs can be made from Waterbury Road or East Fork Road to the campground landing. You can also canoe down from the campground to East Arbutus County Park, on Lake Arbutus. This county park also has a swim beach. The Black River below Lake Arbutus is good for canoeing, but check ahead about water releases from Lake Arbutus. The forest also has numerous lakes for paddling and fishing. Of special note is the Dike 17 Wildlife Area, which is managed for waterfowl. Ducks, geese, and sandhill cranes can be seen from the observation tower. The

Wildcat hiking trails are in the south end of the forest. You may not even mind the drive there because so much of the Black River State Forest is primitive and scenic. If you are very, very, very lucky, you may even see a timber wolf.

East Fork Campground

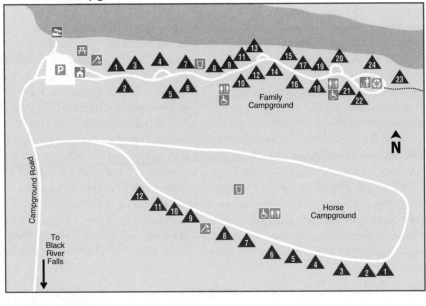

GETTING THERE

From Black River Falls, drive east on WI 54 for 5 miles to County Road K. Turn left on CR K and follow it 5.1 miles to Old State Highway 54. Turn right on Old State Highway 54 and follow it 2 miles to Campground Road. Veer left and follow Campground Road 2 miles to dead-end at East Fork.

GPS COORDINATES: N44° 25.275' W90° 40.567'

15

Harstad County Park Campground

Beauty ★★★ / Privacy ★★★★ / Spaciousness ★★★★★ / Quiet ★★★★ / Security ★★★ / Cleanliness ★★★

This out-of-the-way park is on the Eau Claire River, a great canoeing destination.

By the time I chugged into Harstad Park, the temperature had soared into the 90s. The noon sun was blaring overhead. The only things moving were a few lazy mosquitoes. Sweat poured off me as I set up camp. It was time for a dip in the Eau Claire River, so I walked down to the riverside canoe landing. Bridge Creek flowed shallow into the deep, dark waters of the Eau Claire, forming a large tan sandbar. My toes squished in the sand as I tore off my shirt and splashed into the river. What relief! I spent much of the afternoon on the sandbar, reading beneath a river birch and taking a swim while ol' Sol cranked out the rays.

Harstad Park is definitely an overlooked destination. The amenities aren't immediately obvious on first arrival. While other parks might have a buoyed swim beach with a groomed, grassy lawn for swimmers, Harstad Park has a sandbar at the confluence of Bridge Creek and the Eau Claire River. Instead of a fishing pier, anglers fish from the bank and the canoe landing. This is a place to visit for the simple and rustic pleasure of the outdoors.

The park doesn't harbor any unique physical formations, but the campground lies in an attractive forest. As you enter the campground loop, you'll notice widely branched oaks complemented by jack pines growing over a thick understory. White pine and cherry

The Eau Claire River is the perfect spot to cool off on a hot summer day.   *photographed by Kevin Revolinski*

KEY INFORMATION

CONTACT: Eau Claire County Parks and Forests Department, 715-839-4738 or 715-286-5536, eccountyparks.com

OPEN: Year-round; services available May 15–September 15

SITES: 27

EACH SITE: Picnic table, fire ring, bench

ASSIGNMENT: First come, first served

REGISTRATION: Self-registration on-site

FACILITIES: Vault toilets, pump well

PARKING: At campsites only

FEE: May 15–September 15, $15/night, $75/week; September 16–May 14, $10/night, $50/week

ELEVATION: 925'

RESTRICTIONS:

PETS: On leash only

FIRES: In fire ring only

ALCOHOL: At campsites only

VEHICLES: 2/site

OTHER: 14-day stay limit; quiet hours 11 p.m.–6 a.m.

---

trees also thrive here. Grass generally covers the campsites. Some campsites have concrete benches, while others have wooden benches. The metal fire rings are dug into the ground. Campsites 1–5 are very large but open to the noonday sun. Ascend a rise, and then loop past the wood lot and recycling station. The campground signboard has information on canoe put-ins and takeouts. The next sites are large, too, and even more open to the sun. The openness reveals the bluff upon which the campground rests. However, no campsites offer river views. The oaks crowd in and shade campsites 20–27.

Harstad Park, on the eastern edge of Eau Claire County, is virtually unused during the week, but it can get busy on nice-weather weekends. The pump well is deep, and it can take a little while to get water. Be patient as you pump. Grassy spur trails cut through the center of the woods leading to two vault toilets.

The parkland was donated to Eau Claire County back in 1927 by a fellow named Ole Harstad. The Eau Claire River borders Harstad's land, making this a canoer's park. Much of the Eau Claire here runs through Eau Claire County Forest, giving the river a real wilderness feel. Occasional shoals and rocky rapids add another touch to the paddle. It is but 2 miles from the outflow of Lake Eau Claire to Harstad Park. Many paddlers make the 6-mile run down the Eau Claire from Harstad Park to Big Falls County Park. Big Falls is the most scenic feature of the river, as it descends 15 feet over granite ledges. Do not try to canoe Big Falls! Instead, use the established portage trail. A second day trip runs from Big Falls down to Altoona Lake Park.

At Harstad Park, a groomed day-use area overlooks a noisy river rapid, adding an audible feature to the park. The day-use area houses a large shelter with picnic tables that could be a dry campers' refuge on a rainy day. A horseshoe pit, sandy volleyball court, and playground complement the shelter. If you are looking for more organized action, head to Coon Fork County Park, 8 miles east of Harstad, on County Road 12. Turn left on County Road CF, and follow CR CF to this 80-acre lake with a swim beach, bike trail, fishing pier, and too-busy campground. The park rents paddleboats, rowboats, and canoes on this "no gas motors" impoundment. Anglers fish here for muskellunge, walleye, and smallmouth bass. Though fishing wasn't on the agenda during my visit, the Eau Claire River was a pleasure, especially on that hot day. I hope that it won't be quite so hot during your visit to Harstad Park.

Harstad County Park Campground

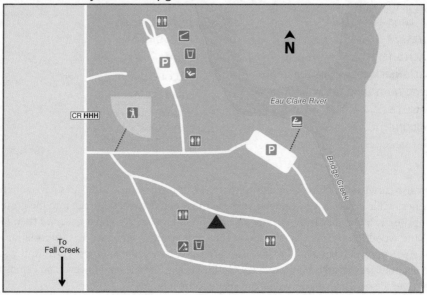

GETTING THERE

From Fall Creek, 9 miles east of Eau Claire, drive east on US 12 for 4.3 miles to County Road AF. Turn left on CR AF and follow it 1.6 miles to County Trunk Highway HHH. Turn left on CTH HHH and follow it 0.3 mile to the county park, on your left.

GPS COORDINATES: N44° 44.261' W91° 10.121'

16

Hartman Creek State Park Campground

Beauty ★★★★ / Privacy ★★★ / Spaciousness ★★★★ / Quiet ★★★★ / Security ★★★★ / Cleanliness ★★★★

This attractive family campground moves as slow as a summer day.

If you want to pass the tent-camping tradition on to your kids, other family members, or friends, take them to Hartman Creek State Park. Camping here is sure to be good, with myriad attractive sites. The campground has showers to break in those less used to roughing it in the great outdoors. And this state park has great outdoor activities—hiking trails, biking trails, and five lakes for your enjoyment. The fishing is good and suitable for both kids and adults. So do a little sweet-talking to the reluctant ones close to you, and after coming to Hartman Creek, they may be the ones urging you to tent camp next time!

The campground is situated along the south side of Allen Lake, an impoundment of Hartman Creek. The campground is laid out in a classic loop with two spur roads. Nearly all the campsites are large, and privacy can be found in the occasional areas of hardwoods (actually remnants of an old apple orchard) amid towering white and red pines over a floor sprinkled with needles. The first 22 sites of the camping area are first come, first served. Campsites 1–16 are in pines with some brushy understory. You'll hit an area of deciduous trees before nearing Allen Lake. Campsites 22, 25, and 28 have lake views from the elevated flat. The loop swings around and climbs a little, staying in the pine zone. The piney sites are preferred, though campsite privacy is often limited.

Here, two crossroads lead left to bisect the loop. The first crossroad leads to sites 75–87. The first few sites in this section are in pines; the rest are in hardwoods for privacy seekers. These sites are also close to the Orchard Shower Building. The second crossroad contains sites 88–100. Thick underbrush in sites 95–100 give privacy, but the sites are open to the sun overhead.

The main loop continues around to reach sites 39–74. Most of these are in the pines. Some sites on the outside of the loop are backed against a hill. The Pine Shower Building is located near campsite 44, as is the campground host. Campsites 54–64 are underneath the hardwoods. The last 10 sites are open under the pines.

Emmons Creek flows just south of the park. *photographed by Kevin Revolinski*

KEY INFORMATION

CONTACT: Wisconsin Department of Natural Resources, 715-258-2372, tinyurl.com /HartmanCreek; reservations 888-WI-PARKS, wisconsin.goingtocamp.com

OPEN: May–October

SITES: 79 primitive, 23 electric

EACH SITE: Picnic table, fire grate

ASSIGNMENT: By phone; internet; or first come, first served

REGISTRATION: At entrance station

FACILITIES: Hot showers, flush toilets, pit toilets, water spigots

PARKING: At campsites only

FEE: Wisconsin residents, $18 ($30 electric site); nonresidents, $23 ($35 electric site); plus vehicle admission fee (Wisconsin residents, $8; nonresidents, $11; Wisconsin residents age 65 and older, $3); $7.75 reservation fee

ELEVATION: 925'

RESTRICTIONS:

PETS: On leash only and not allowed at beach or picnic area

FIRES: In fire ring only; firewood must be purchased in state within 25 miles of campground

ALCOHOL: At campsites only

VEHICLES: 2/site

OTHER: 14-day stay limit

Hartman Creek will fill on nice summer weekends. However, campsites 22–100 are reservable, so call ahead and start relaxing early.

The park is blessed with numerous lakes. Allen Lake, near the campground, is fun for kids and adults for catching panfish and bass. Deer Path Trail circles the lake, making for easy access. A fishing pier makes angling even easier. Hartman Lake has a 300-foot swim beach with a grassy shoreline and shaded areas too. Marl Lake, Pope Lake, and Manomin Lake can be accessed from the Whispering Pines Picnic Area.

The Ice Age Trail, Wisconsin's premier long-distance path, makes part of its extended trek through Hartman Creek. Three miles of the trail pass directly through the park. Far-away Valley, along Emmons Creek just south of the park, is especially scenic. The trail keeps on for 9 miles north beyond the park border. However, there are plenty of trails inside the park. You can make a near loop on the Dike Trail. Mountain bikers and hikers share the Glacial Bike Loop and the Windfelt Trail. Oak Ridge Trail is for hikers only. Pope Lake Trail makes a 1-mile loop through the pines.

All of the above are only suggested activities. You may just want to tool around the campground on your bike or pedal the park roads. Better yet, you may want to sit around the fire and pass on those all-important fishing tips to the next generation. After a few adventures at Hartman Lake, they will be carrying on the tent-camping tradition at this fine state park.

Hartman Creek State Park Campground

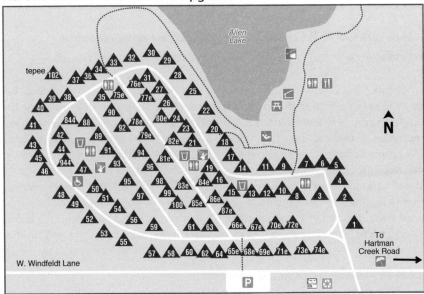

GETTING THERE

From Waupaca and the junction of US 10 and WI 54, take WI 54 west 4.4 miles to Hartman Creek Road. Turn left on Hartman Creek Road and drive 2 miles to enter the park.

GPS COORDINATES: N44° 19.426' W89° 12.995'

17

Lake Wissota State Park Campground

Beauty ★★★ / Privacy ★★★★ / Spaciousness ★★★ / Quiet ★★ / Security ★★★★★ / Cleanliness ★★★

You will be surprised at the combination of developed and rustic recreation opportunities here.

Lake Wissota State Park is close to the city of Chippewa Falls—too close I feared, before coming to check it out. But after overnighting here, I came to appreciate its rustic nature despite its proximity to town. On the shores of big Lake Wissota, the park offers the watery recreation associated with a big lake, yet also has lots of trails for hikers and mountain bikers in a restored prairie. The campground is heavily wooded and well kept and offers a great natural respite for tent campers, including those from Chippewa Falls and Eau Claire. It's a good sign when locals use a campground just minutes from home.

The campground is set on a bluff well above Lake Wissota and is divided into two bisected loops. The first loop contains sites 1–60. A campground host fronts the first loop. Basswood, white pines, maples, and oaks loom overhead. Thick brush not only divides the

Wildflowers line the trails at Lake Wissota State Park.

photographed by Amy Bayer/Flickr/CC BY-ND 2.0 (creativecommons.org/licenses/by-nd/2.0)

KEY INFORMATION

CONTACT: Wisconsin Department of Natural Resources, 715-382-4574, tinyurl.com/LakeWissotaSP; reservations 888-WI-PARKS, wisconsin.goingtocamp.com

OPEN: Year-round; water available from last frost of spring to first frost of fall

SITES: 58 primitive, 58 electric

EACH SITE: Picnic table, fire ring

ASSIGNMENT: By phone; internet; or first come, first served

REGISTRATION: At visitor center

FACILITIES: Hot showers, flush toilets, pit toilets, water spigots

PARKING: At campsites only

FEE: Wisconsin residents, $20 ($30 electric site); nonresidents, $25 ($35 electric site); plus vehicle admission fee (Wisconsin residents, $8; nonresidents, $11; Wisconsin residents age 65 and older, $3); $7.75 reservation fee

ELEVATION: 950′

RESTRICTIONS:

PETS: On leash only

FIRES: In fire ring only; firewood must be purchased in state within 25 miles of campground

ALCOHOL: At campsites only

VEHICLES: 2/site

OTHER: 14-day stay limit

---

sites but also often runs along the paved campground road, adding extra privacy. The electric sites are distributed throughout both loops. Some recommended sites here include 11, 15, 17, 19, and 40. Campsites closest to the lake are 24–36. You can sense the lake's presence, but thick woods prevent lake views. Also, the Lake Trail runs between the campsites and the edge of the bluff.

A field and playground with a shelter nearby lie between the two loops. The second loop holds campsites 61–116. The first few sites are a little too open, but the woods thicken as you near the lake. Sites 68–79 are closest to the lake, and the trail that runs behind the outside of the loop runs 0.5 mile to the beach. Beyond the turn at 81, the loop enters a red pine plantation. It offers very large sites with pine needles for a floor, but there's no campsite privacy due to a lack of understory brush. Lake Wissota is a busy park during the summer. Reservations are recommended on weekends, and all campsites are now reservable.

Water is the star of the show here. Boaters of all stripes use the park. Campers and day users flock to the large swim beach, located on an arm of 6,300-acre Lake Wissota. A picnic area and bathhouse are located at the beach. Also near here is a boat landing that can accommodate most any boat a camper would bring. Canoes and kayaks are for rent in case you are boatless. A fishing pier, along with a few other access points scattered throughout the park, enables shore anglers to try their luck. Anglers most often go for walleye and smallmouth bass here, but muskie, pike, largemouth bass, panfish, and catfish are also caught.

If you are going to hike only one trail here, take the 1-mile Beaver Meadow Nature Trail. I enjoyed this path that travels through a marsh and offers interpretive information along the way. Most campers like the Lake Trail because it runs directly on the bluff overlooking Lake Wissota and connects to the campground. The Staghorn Trail is 2 miles long and, like the previous trails, is hiker-only. Mountain bikers have many other paths available (11 miles worth) that are also open to hikers and horses. The terrain is mostly level, but the prairie and woods scenery will keep your eyes plenty busy, instead of looking down for roots and rocks. Bikers also ply park roads and the paved campground loops.

If the trails of Wissota State Park aren't enough for you, try out the Old Abe State Trail. This 20-mile paved rail-trail runs north to reach Brunet Island State Park (see page 101). People like to hike, bike, and even inline-skate this path that runs through agricultural and forest land beside the Chippewa River. To reach the southern terminus of the Old Abe Trail, turn left from the park onto County Road O, and follow it for 2 miles to the trailhead at the intersection of CR O and CR S. You can just bike from the park, since CR O was widened to enable bike access from the park. With the town of Chippewa Falls so near, why not take advantage of it? Supplies are close by, and you might consider touring the Leinenkugel Brewery. One of Wisconsin's most notable labels has been brewing beer since 1878.

Lake Wissota State Park Campground

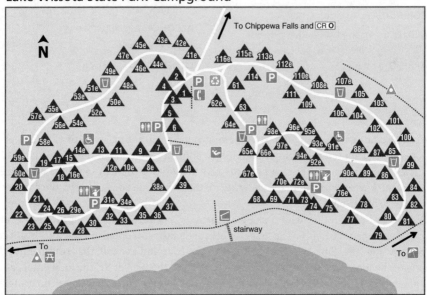

GETTING THERE

From downtown Chippewa Falls, take WI 178 east 3 miles to County Road S. Turn right on CR S and follow it 2.2 miles to CR O. Turn right on CR O and follow it 2 miles to the park, on your right.

GPS COORDINATES: N44° 58.176' W91° 17.926'

18

Mirror Lake State Park Campground

Beauty ★★★★ / Privacy ★★★ / Spaciousness ★★★★ / Quiet ★★★ / Security ★★★★ / Cleanliness ★★★★

The picturesque lake, nearly 2,000 acres of forest, and 20 miles of hiking trails make up this park, which is a welcome contrast to the tourist trade at nearby Wisconsin Dells.

As you look out at the sandstone cliffs above the lake, you are looking back in time 500 million years to the Cambrian period, when this was all under the sea. The gorge that Mirror Lake occupies was formed quite suddenly in geological terms, when a glacial lake burst forth from its ice dam at the end of the most recent ice age and rushed through the soft rock. A dam on Dell Creek created this lake, and the protective sandstone cliffs keep the waters still and give them that reflective character from which the lake takes its name. The picturesque lake, nearly 2,000 acres of forest, and 20 miles of hiking trails make up this park, which is a welcome contrast to the tourist trade at nearby Wisconsin Dells.

Looking down on Mirror Lake from the hiking trail   *photographed by Kevin Revolinski*

Three campgrounds run along the eastern side of the lake, which runs north–south. Check in at the office and visitor center, and follow the main road past the entrances to all three.

Bluewater Bay is the first of the bunch, offering 57 sites, 42 of which can be reserved. The best sites are the tent-camping-only sites 301–307 on the north side of the campground. No vehicles are allowed here, and the sites are quite private and spacious, set back beyond the first parking lot to the right as you enter Bluewater Bay. Because the rest of the sites are south of the entry road and divided in four loops, starting from the main road and leading to the lake, there is no traffic distraction here.

Just past the tent-only site parking area are the shower facility and flush toilets, as well as some playground equipment. Each of the other loops has its own water source and shares pit toilets with the neighboring loop. Sites 45–57 are in the loop closest to the water and farthest in, though none of the sites has a view of the lake. Sites 55 and 57 are less shaded than the others, but all are rather spacious and granted privacy by surrounding brush.

The other three loops are roughly the same, with the proximity to the showers near the first loop (sites 1–15) being the most significant difference. Sites 31 and 32 in the third loop

KEY INFORMATION

CONTACT: Wisconsin Department of Natural Resources, 608-254-2333, tinyurl.com/MirrorLakeSP; reservations 888-WI-PARKS, wisconsin.goingtocamp.com

OPEN: Year-round

SITES: 104 primitive, 47 electric, 4 walk-in

EACH SITE: Picnic table, fire pit, lantern hook, sand or gravel pad

ASSIGNMENT: By phone; internet; or first come, first served

REGISTRATION: At park office; in off-season, at office or self-register

FACILITIES: Showers, flush toilets, pit toilets, water, pay phones

PARKING: At campsites only

FEE: Wisconsin residents, $22 ($32 electric site); nonresidents, $27 ($37 electric site); plus vehicle admission fee (Wisconsin residents, $8; nonresidents, $11; Wisconsin residents age 65 and older, $3); $7.75 reservation fee

ELEVATION: 874′

RESTRICTIONS:

PETS: On leash only

FIRES: In fire pit only; firewood must be purchased in state within 25 miles of campground

ALCOHOL: At campsites only

VEHICLES: 2/site

---

trade more space for less privacy. The first and second loops lose some of the scrub brush, so your neighbors are visible though comfortably distant.

Sandstone Ridge is the second campground, and though better suited for RVs, this is the only section that remains open for winter camping. Walk-in sites 201–204 are off the main loop and centered on a small parking area. Because of a lack of brush between sites, they lack the privacy you might expect. Sites 83 and 84 are the best options and have a limited view of the lake. Along the section 89–96 you can expect a bit of sunshine, and of these sites, the last two are best for tents.

Canoes, boats, and bikes can be rented at the beach down a trail from the end of this campground. Flush toilets and showers serve Sandstone Ridge well.

Cliffwood Campground offers views of the lake from sites 135–138, but these sites are less private than in the other camps. In fact, sites 106–121 come in pairs, so they would be better suited for larger groups. Sites 123–125 on the little loop to the right are nicely shaded, shielded from general traffic, and put at least 50 feet between neighboring sites. The pit toilets are on the other side of the main road opposite this section, and a water spigot is at either end of this little half loop.

The road to the beach and parking area there is just past Bluewater Bay Campground. The boat landing, fishing pier, and a shoreline boardwalk are down a different access road. Turn into the Sandstone Ridge Campground and take the first road to the right down to a parking area. Canoe and bike rentals can be had here, and you can pick up your firewood and ice at the concession stand as well.

The lake, placid and perfect for a day's paddling, is the obvious star of the park. Sandstone cliffs rise up as much as 50 feet from the reflective waters. But the park also has 20 miles of hiking trails through the pine and oak woods that surround the lake. Follow Echo Rock hiking trail out of Cliffwood Campground to find an excellent scenic overlook. A portion of this trail is also accessible for wheelchairs. Heading south from Bluewater Bay Campground, take the East Loop hiking trail to cross to the other side of the southern spike of the lake. Trails dedicated to bikers are south of Fern Dell Road. Winter campers should pack cross-country skis or snowshoes or consider an old Wisconsin standby: ice fishing.

Mirror Lake State Park Campground

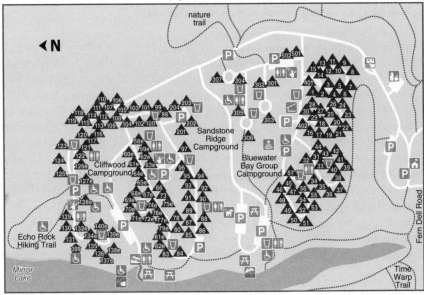

GETTING THERE

From I-90/94 at Exit 92 near Baraboo, take US 12 south to Fern Dell Road. Go west 1.5 miles to the park entrance.

GPS COORDINATES: N43° 33.677' W89° 48.485'

19

Perrot State Park Campground

Beauty ★★★ / Privacy ★★★ / Spaciousness ★★★★ / Quiet ★★★★ / Security ★★★ / Cleanliness ★★★★

Enjoy both hilly and watery environments at this state park.

The land upon which Perrot State Park lies has been popular for a long, long time. This upper–Mississippi River Valley area of bluffs, thick forests, deep valleys, and flowing waters was first occupied by mound-building ancients as far back as 7,000 years ago. Later, French voyageur Nicholas Perrot made a winter camp here in 1685 while building trade with the Dakota and Iowa tribes. In 1731 a French fort was built on this very site. Fast-forward to 1927, when the scenic spot was taken over by the state of Wisconsin and built into a park that offers land- and water-based recreation, as well as a nice spot to pitch your tent.

The campground matches the park's natural beauty. It offers both electric and nonelectric sites on hilly terrain. Tent campers should know that the electric areas are generally congregated together, keeping the big rigs separate from the good campsites. Enter the campground and immediately reach the main electric loop (sites 1–23). These sites are well spaced apart but are usually filled with RVs. Fear not; drive right and reach a spur road heading left to access the loop with campsites 51–86. This spur road bisects the loop and has the best sites (51–59). Hilly terrain and heavy vegetation offer private sites beneath a

The Voyageurs Canoe Trail makes a loop around Trempealeau Bay and features spectacular views of Trempealeau Mountain. *photographed by Kevin Revolinski*

KEY INFORMATION

CONTACT: 608-534-6409, tinyurl.com
/perrotSP; reservations 888-WI-PARKS,
wisconsin.goingtocamp.com

OPEN: Mid-April–mid-October

SITES: 62 primitive, 36 electric

EACH SITE: Picnic table, fire ring

ASSIGNMENT: By phone; internet;
or first come, first served

REGISTRATION: At ranger station

FACILITIES: Hot showers, flush toilets,
pit toilets, water spigots

PARKING: At campsites only

FEE: Wisconsin residents, $20 ($30 electric
site); nonresidents, $25 ($35 electric site);
plus vehicle admission fee (Wisconsin
residents, $8; nonresidents, $11;
Wisconsin residents age 65 and older, $3);
$7.75 reservation fee

ELEVATION: 675'

RESTRICTIONS:

PETS: On 8-foot leash only

FIRES: In fire ring only; firewood must be
purchased in state within 25 miles of
campground

ALCOHOL: At campsites only

VEHICLES: 2/site

OTHER: 14-day stay limit

---

shady hardwood forest. Campsites 61–69 offer a mix of sun and shade with pine, sumac, and hickory trees. The sites are well separated. Campsites 70–86 start out with too much sun but then become completely shaded after campsite 75.

If you head left instead of right at the main electric loop, you'll come to sites 30–50. Of these, 36–48 are the most coveted in all the park, as they offer a view of Trempealeau Bay in an ever-expanding woodland (40, 42, 46, and 48 are opposite the road from the water). Because of said lake view, there is an extra charge of $3 per night on sites 36–38, 41, and 43-45. Beyond here is a miniloop with several sites: 24–27 are on a small miniloop and are too sloped for a good night's sleep; 28 and 29 are electric and should be bypassed. A final area houses the upper sites, which number 87–95 and are second in demand to those on Trempealeau Bay. These sites are widespread, like the entire campground, and shaded by white pines. You can access the Great River State Trail near here.

Perrot will fill on most Saturday nights during summer. You can generally squeeze in on Friday night, save for holiday weekends. I suggest eliminating the worry and calling ahead, since all sites are reservable. Water, showers, and toilets are spread throughout the campground.

Hiking is popular here. Seven miles of hiking paths cruise along the river and to heights such as Brady's Bluff, where you can gain a good view of your camping paradise. Another view can be had on Perrot Ridge. The Black Walnut Nature Trail makes its loop near rock formations and in deep woods. For a lower, more watery perspective, take the 2.5-mile Riverview Trail. Seven miles of other trails are open to mountain bikers and hikers. The main path starts near park headquarters and makes several smaller loops before returning to the park office. The major attraction for bikers is the Great River State Trail. This 24-mile rail-trail starts in North La Crosse and travels through the upper Mississippi River Valley amid prairie and bottomland. The trail traverses 20 bridges, including the 287-foot trestle over the Black River. It also passes by some Hopewell Indian mounds before entering the Upper Mississippi Wildlife Refuge, home to eagles. Perrot State Park offers a spur path connecting to the Great River State Trail directly from the campground.

Other attractions include canoeing Trempealeau Bay. The Voyageurs Canoe Trail starts at the park canoe launch and makes a 3.4-mile loop around the bay, offering great views of Trempealeau Mountain. The French word *trempealeau* roughly translates to "mountain in the water," and you will see that this is true. Anglers can catch anything from pike to bass to crappie to walleye to panfish. The park has a boat launch in lower Trempealeau Bay. Another way to enjoy the water is at the town of Trempealeau's public pool. Perrot State Park nature center is also by the river and houses information on archaeology, fish, and the mound builders of the region. Your history lesson here, along with a little exploration of your own, will make clear why this location has been popular for thousands of years.

Perrot State Park Campground

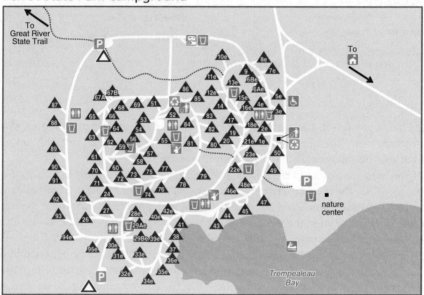

GETTING THERE

From I-90 near La Crosse, take Exit 4 to US 53. Head north on US 53 for 9 miles to WI 35. Turn left on WI 35 and follow it 8 miles into the town of Trempealeau. Turn left on Main Street and follow it 0.1 mile to Park Road. Turn right on First Street and follow it to enter the park.

GPS COORDINATES: N44° 00.758' W91° 27.733'

20

Pigeon Creek Campground

Beauty ★★★★ / Privacy ★★★★ / Spaciousness: ★★★★ / Quiet ★★ / Security ★★★ / Cleanliness ★★★★★

Pigeon Creek is the most underutilized campground in this entire guidebook.

Campgrounds located within quick driving access from an interstate are often overcrowded with RVs and overrun in general. Pigeon Creek bucks that trend. Located just a few miles off I-94 near Black River Falls, this destination within the Black River State Forest is actually underutilized. Sure, it gets a few travelers wandering off the interstate, but the lack of hookups or showers keeps the big-rig set away for the most part. This campground offers a near-ideal setting for tent campers and has all sorts of fun stuff to do nearby, yet it won't even fill on July 4. Frankly, I'm stumped as to why!

But never mind the whys. Just appreciate the fact that you can throw your tent in the car, hit I-94, and be guaranteed a campsite! And once you come here, you will be coming back for more. Folks who discover Pigeon Creek become regulars who swear by the place. The campground is situated in an attractive forest near Pigeon Creek Flowage, a dark-water impoundment (Pigeon Creek is just a little stream that feeds the lake). Enter the paved campground loop road to beautiful white pine stands mixed with mostly maple trees. Oaks, aspens, and jack pines are also represented. Ferns, brush, and young trees between campsites make for ample camp-site privacy. Campsites are also spaced well apart from one another. Furthermore, you most likely won't have any neighbors camping beside you! The only drawback I see—er, hear—is the low hum of cars from I-94, but I didn't find it bothersome during any of my three stays here.

Explorers will find plenty of trails at Black River State Forest. *photographed by Kevin Revolinski*

The main loop contains sites 1–29. Pass the pump well at the loop's beginning, and then pass many great campsites. Most are well shaded and have a grass or sand floor to make staking your tent a breeze. A giant white pine grows near campsite 1. Another majestic pine shades campsite 7. A miniloop spurs off the main loop past campsite 10 and houses campsites 30–38. Campsite 34 is at the back of the miniloop. Wooden barriers separate the parking spur from the camping area. Back on the main loop, campsites 12, 14, 18, and 20 have pull-through parking. Most sites on the outside of the loop are above average in size. The last two sites, 27 and 29, are the most popular because they are closest to the water. A pump well and two pairs of vault toilets serve the campground.

KEY INFORMATION

CONTACT: Wisconsin Department of Natural Resources, 715-284-4103, tinyurl.com/BlackRiverSF; reservations 888-WI-PARKS, wisconsin.goingtocamp.com

OPEN: May 15–October 1

SITES: 38

EACH SITE: Picnic table, fire grate

ASSIGNMENT: By phone; internet; or first come, first served

REGISTRATION: At ranger station or self-registration on-site

FACILITIES: Vault toilets, pump well

PARKING: At campsites only

FEE: Wisconsin residents, $18; nonresidents, $23; plus vehicle admission fee (Wisconsin residents, $8; nonresidents, $11; Wisconsin residents age 65 and older, $3); $7.75 reservation fee

ELEVATION: 950'

RESTRICTIONS:

PETS: On leash only

FIRES: In fire ring only; firewood must be purchased in state within 25 miles of campground

ALCOHOL: At campsites only

VEHICLES: 2/site

OTHER: Use of generators prohibited

The 34-acre Pigeon Creek Flowage is mostly bordered in brush and grass. While bass, panfish, and catfish call it home, the flowage is not a destination for serious anglers. Geared more toward family fun, the lake is quiet (thanks to the "nonmotorized only" rule) and is a perfect place for kids to explore by canoe. The lake also enjoys one of the largest swim beaches in the state parks and forests; the sloped sandy shore is nearly 100 yards wide and leads up to a grassy picnic area with scattered shade trees, picnic tables, and grills. The lake is fairly shallow and good for swimming. A grassy "island" connected by a narrow peninsula lies in the middle of the lake. Yet another swimming experience can be had at Robinson Beach, just a short car trip away. Robinson Beach is an old quarry now filled with crystal-clear groundwater. This beach also has a picnic area.

Mountain bikers will really enjoy this campground. The Pigeon Creek Mountain Bike Trail leaves directly from the campground, passes over Pigeon Creek Flowage dam, and then heads right 1.8 miles to North Settlement Road and left 2.9 miles to Smrekar Road. Just 0.5 mile on Smrekar Road is the Smrekar Mountain Biking and Cross-Country Ski Trails parking area. Combined with the Wildcat Trails on the north side of North Settlement Road, fat-tire enthusiasts have more than 24 miles of paths to pedal! Hikers often use these trails, too, and lucky wildlife viewers may spot members of the elk herd re-introduced to the state forest in 2015, 2016, and 2017. Backpackers will tent camp at Pigeon Creek Campground, and then take off on overnight treks in this loop-laden trail system. Whether you are backpacking or not, toss your tent in the car and head out on a camping trek at Pigeon Creek.

Pigeon Creek Campground

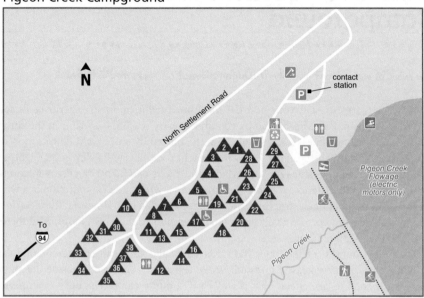

GETTING THERE

From Exit 128 on I-94, head east on County Road O for 0.3 mile. Turn left on North Settlement Road and follow it 2 miles to the campground, on your right.

GPS COORDINATES: N44° 12.673' W90° 37.048'

21

Point Beach State Forest Campground

Beauty ★★★ / Privacy ★★★★ / Spaciousness ★★★★ / Quiet ★★★ / Security ★★★★ / Cleanliness ★★★★

Six miles of waterfront on Lake Michigan attract campers to Point Beach.

Point Beach State Forest is your best bet for a beachfront camping experience in south-eastern Wisconsin. Point Beach can be cool in the early season, busy later in the summer, and mosquito-ish at times, but a stroll along the tan sands on Lake Michigan more than compensates for any of these ills. From the beach, you will see Rawley Point Lighthouse, a century-old beacon to ships on Lake Michigan. Hikers and bikers can enjoy inland trails totaling 10 miles in distance. A word of caution: As a whole, the campground is a winner, but the sheer number of electric campsites brings in the big rigs. However, the electric sites are generally segregated, effectively leaving tent campers to their own loops. And there are some great tent-camping sites here.

The campground sits back about 100 yards from Lake Michigan, situated on undulating old dunes that are now heavily forested. While it may not be directly beside the shore, it does get the cooling lake effect. That is why early summer can be less busy—campers fear

A visit to Rawley Point Lighthouse is a highlight at Point Beach State Forest.

photographed by Preamtip Satasuk

KEY INFORMATION

CONTACT: Wisconsin Department of Natural Resources, 920-794-7480, tinyurl.com /PointBeachSF; reservations 888-WI-PARKS, wisconsin.goingtocamp.com

OPEN: Year-round; water available from last frost of spring to first frost of fall

SITES: 57 primitive, 70 electric

EACH SITE: Picnic table, fire ring

ASSIGNMENT: By phone; internet; or first come, first served

REGISTRATION: At visitor center

FACILITIES: Hot showers, flush toilets, pit toilets, water spigots

PARKING: At campsites only

FEE: Wisconsin residents, $22 ($32 electric site); nonresidents, $27 ($37 electric site); plus vehicle admission fee (Wisconsin residents, $8; nonresidents, $11; Wisconsin residents age 65 and older, $3); $7.75 registration fee

ELEVATION: 600'

RESTRICTIONS:

PETS: On leash only

FIRES: In fire ring only; firewood must be purchased in state within 25 miles of campground

ALCOHOL: At campsites only

VEHICLES: 2/site

OTHER: 14-day stay limit; 6 people/site

---

a freeze-out. A paved park road lies between the lake and the campground, but fortunately for campers, thick evergreens and underbrush mostly screen the road.

On first inspection, the campground seems like a maze. The first loop houses sites 1–16. It offers widely separated sites with thick brush between them in an oak–white pine forest. These are first-come, first-serve sites. The next loop offers sites 17–30. It is a little too close to the main park road, has a few electric sites mixed in, and is not recommended. Next comes the loop that offers the best in tent camping at Point Beach. Remember this loop for reservations: 31–62. Pass the campground shower area, and enter a narrow road that specifically forbids RVs. This narrow road twists and undulates beneath a pretty forest of sugar maples, birches, oaks, and white pines. The sites are widely spaced and have thick brush between them, offering good campsite privacy. Some of the sites have fences, prohibiting vehicles from driving up or down a hill to reach the actual site, effectively making them walk-in campsites. Both sides of the loop have good sites, and due to the twisting road and elevation changes, there is a variety of sites and situations. You won't go wrong choosing any of the sites; although, after your first visit, you may find one you prefer for next time. During the week, the campground often doesn't fill; just come and take your chances.

With a few exceptions, sites 63–125 are electric. Of special note are 120, a nonelectric site offering solitude, and 119, which is near the Ridges Trail. The electric sites are strung out on a long loop that is nicely forested, but I prefer to stay away from the big rigs with the lights strung on them like it was Christmas. The electric sites are first to fill. Make reservations after mid-June through mid-August if coming on a weekend. Remember, the mosquitoes can be troublesome here. Many campers bring screen shelters. Most campsites can accommodate a screen shelter, tent, and other gear. The lodge, located near the entrance station, serves hamburgers and such.

The beach is the big draw here. Six miles of lakefront give beachcombers plenty of room to crunch their feet as clear, cool Lake Michigan laps against the shoreline. Swimmers can tackle the chilly waters, but be advised that lifeguards are not provided. Try to get up to watch the sunrise from the beach—it's quite a sight. Everyone enjoys visiting Rawley Point Lighthouse. The original brick lighthouse was built in 1853. It was later cut down and made into the lightkeeper's house. The second tower was built in 1894, and at 113 feet it is one of the largest and brightest on the Great Lakes. Other sights can be seen on the forest's 2,900 acres. Campers can pedal along the campground and forest roads, but they should be careful, as the roads can get busy on warm weekends. A bicycle trail plies the inland woods. The hiking trails loop south from the campground all the way to Molash Creek. The Red Pine Trail makes a 3-mile loop inland from the campground. The Ice Age National Scenic Trail enters from the north, passes through the trail system, and continues south along the shore into Two Rivers. Equestrian enthusiasts can ride 2.3 miles of trails as well. You will enjoy these trails, but like most tent campers, you will be enjoying all that sand on Lake Michigan.

Point Beach State Forest Campground

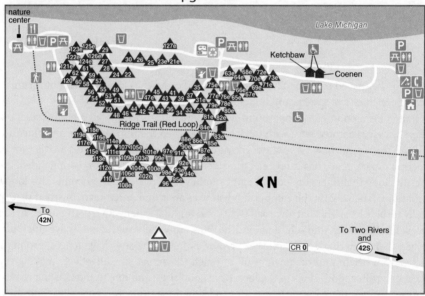

GETTING THERE

From Two Rivers, drive north on County Road O 5 miles to reach the forest, on your left.

GPS COORDINATES: N44° 12.981' W87° 10.546'

22

Roche-A-Cri State Park Campground

Beauty ★★★★ / Privacy ★★★ / Spaciousness ★★★★ / Quiet ★★ / Security ★★★★ / Cleanliness ★★★

This is the nearest reasonably peaceful tent campground within driving distance of the Wisconsin Dells.

Roche-A-Cri is quite a landmark on the Wisconsin landscape, as is the state park that surrounds and protects it. Roche-A-Cri itself is a rock prominence uplifting from the central Wisconsin landscape. Its 300-foot elevation allows a view of 10 counties and up to 60 miles away! First discovered by aboriginals who left petroglyphs to prove their find, the flat-topped cliff-sided perch was dubbed the crying rock by Frenchmen. Later, American soldiers and explorers let their presence be known with their own rock inscriptions. Today, visitors can camp in an attractive, wooded campground at the base of Roche-A-Cri, get a view from the top, and make their own memory that needs no inscription. The park's proximity to the Wisconsin Dells, 30 miles south, makes for a sane base camp and respite to explore the tourist madness that is the Dells.

Before you hit the Dells or climb the 303 wooden steps to the top of Roche-A-Cri, find a site at the campground. Your biggest problem will be choosing from the many ideal tent sites. The campground is laid out in a classic loop, with a side road splitting the loop in half. Tall pines and oaks shade the loop. Smaller trees and thick brush provide ample campsite privacy. Enter the loop, and pass a pump well. Immediately appreciate the large, mostly level sites. A bathroom building lies on the inside of the loop after campsite 7. Just past here is a handicapped-accessible site with electricity, and then the loop begins to turn away from WI 13. A side road containing eight ultrashady sites splits the main loop. A small, sandy play area lies near here.

The west part of the loop, with sites 26–41, curves toward the base of Roche-A-Cri. Some of the sites against the base of the outcrop are sloped, but most are level and have the added scenery of red pines, jack pines, and boulders as their backyard.

The only drawback here? Roche-A-Cri was a state holding that started as a roadside park, and then expanded to become a state park. In a sense it still is a roadside park, since WI 13 is within earshot for the first half of the loop. An upside is campsite availability—Roche-A-Cri fills only on

The park's namesake

photographed by Preamtip Satasuk

KEY INFORMATION

CONTACT: Wisconsin Department of Natural Resources, summer 608-339-6881, November–April 608-565-2789, tinyurl.com /RocheACri; reservations 888-WI-PARKS, wisconsin.goingtocamp.com

OPEN: May–mid-October

SITES: 37 primitive, 4 electric

EACH SITE: Picnic table, fire grate, wood bench

ASSIGNMENT: By phone; internet; or first come, first served

REGISTRATION: At park office or self-registration if office is closed

FACILITIES: Vault toilets, pump well

PARKING: At campsites only

FEE: Wisconsin residents, $16 ($28 electric site); nonresidents, $21 ($33 electric site); plus vehicle admission fee (Wisconsin residents, $8; nonresidents, $11; Wisconsin residents age 65 and older, $3); $7.75 reservation fee

ELEVATION: 1,000'

RESTRICTIONS:

PETS: On leash only

FIRES: In fire ring only; firewood must be purchased in state within 25 miles of campground

ALCOHOL: At campsites only

VEHICLES: 2/site

OTHER: 14-day stay limit

summer holiday weekends. All sites are reservable. Showers can be had 2 miles south in Friendship. Check the park office for shower sites and directions.

Some great trails are walkable directly from the campground. The Acorn Trail circumnavigates Roche-A-Cri Mound and passes amid some thick and open forests along the way. It also passes Chickadee Rock, a neat formation, but the rock lacks a view. In the fields of the Turkey Vulture Trail, you can see these big carrion-eating birds drifting between Roche-A-Cri and Friendship Mound, 0.5 mile south. For some vertical variation, make the climb to the top of Roche-A-Cri. Plaques atop the outcrop tell you exactly what you are looking at in the distance. This is the sheerest rock face in Wisconsin, left standing after the waters of ancient Glacial Lake Wisconsin broke from their ice dam at the end of the most recent ice age. The campground road and the 1-mile paved loop around Roche-A-Cri make for fun and casual bicycling. Carter Creek, a good trout stream, is within walking distance to the campground. This watercourse has been manipulated to make it a better habitat for fish. Friendship Lake, 1.5 miles south of the park, has a nice swim beach for cooling off on a hot day. The park office loans out handheld GPS units that are preloaded with geocaches both here and at Buckhorn State Park.

And then there are the Wisconsin Dells. Love it or hate it, the area is a draw. Here, you can float the Wisconsin River on a double-decker boat or a "duck," an amphibious boat that traverses both land and water. And the man-made amusements are endless. After a hectic day down at the Dells, you will really appreciate the sanity and serenity found at Roche-A-Cri.

Roche-A-Cri State Park Campground

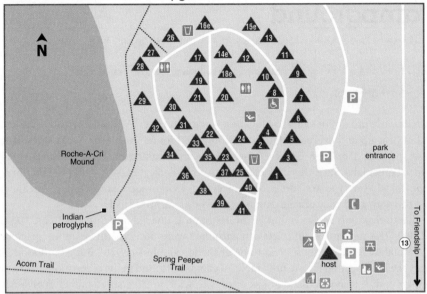

GETTING THERE

From Friendship, head north on WI 13 for 2 miles to the park, on your left.

GPS COORDINATES: N44° 00.058' W89° 48.793'

23

Willow River State Park Campground

Beauty ★★★★ / Privacy ★★★★★ / Spaciousness ★★★ / Quiet ★★★ / Security ★★★ / Cleanliness ★★★

Willow Falls and a high-quality campground will surprise visitors at this Twin Cities getaway.

With its close proximity to the Twin Cities, you might expect Willow River State Park to be kind of beat-up and overused. Quite the contrary. I found more than 3,000 acres of well-preserved land here in St. Croix County, with a great campground set on the shores of a large yet quiet lake. Sure, this park can get busy, but dedicated park staffers keep it in good shape. So whether you are into waterfall viewing, swimming, hiking, fishing, or canoeing, head this way, grab your private campsite, and be as surprised as I was.

This state park is a winner, but be aware that it is divided into three sections: 100, 200, and 300. The newer 100 and 200 campgrounds were designed to be more spacious to accommodate RVs, and these tend to be unshaded and less private. But a bluff atop Little Falls Lake is the setting for the preferable 70 campsites found in the older, more mature 300 campground. A lush woodland of oak trees with widespread gnarled branches gives shade to this campground, plus some basswood and brush give the campground the maximum privacy rating. The campground loop has two crossroads. A red pine plantation shades the

Families frolic in the falls at Willow River. *courtesy of Wisconsin Department of Tourism*

KEY INFORMATION

CONTACT: Wisconsin Department of Natural Resources, 715-386-5931, tinyurl.com /WillowRiverSP; reservations 888-WI-PARKS, wisconsin.goingtocamp.com

OPEN: Year-round; water and showers on from last frost of spring to first frost of fall

SITES: 129 primitive, 25 electric

EACH SITE: Picnic table, fire ring

ASSIGNMENT: By phone; internet; or first come, first served

REGISTRATION: At entrance station

FACILITIES: Hot showers, flush toilets, pit toilets, water spigots

PARKING: At campsites only

FEE: Wisconsin residents, $20 ($35 electric site); nonresidents, $25 ($40 electric site); plus vehicle admission fee (Wisconsin residents, $10; nonresidents, $13; Wisconsin residents age 65 and older, $3); $7.75 reservation fee

ELEVATION: 825'

RESTRICTIONS:

PETS: On leash only

FIRES: In fire ring only; firewood must be purchased in state within 25 miles of campground

ALCOHOL: At campsites

VEHICLES: 2/site

OTHER: 14-day stay limit

---

southeastern part of the loop, but it is the only part of the campground that lacks a thick understory. The piney campsites have needles for a floor and an airiness not found at the rest of the heavily vegetated campground.

As you enter the 300 campground, you'll see campsites 301–306 straight ahead, located on one of the crossroads. The very thickness of the forest here barely allows a car to enter the campsites from the narrow but paved campground road. This narrow road discourages the big rigs, too, although some pop-up campers will be found, especially on the electric sites on the inside of the loop. The main loop circles the bluff's edge overlooking Little Falls Lake, an impoundment of Willow River. Many campsites are perched along the edge of the bluff. Most every site here is desirable. Recommended reservable bluff-side campsites include 317, 319, 352, 354, and 356. While part of the loop away from the lake has many fine secluded sites, avoid sites 327–328, 369–370, and 366–367, as you may end up on a double site. Other recommended reservable sites not along the lake are 307, 309, 312, and 361.

The second crossroad includes campsites 321–326. Most of these sites are electric. The most important part of this crossroad is the shower facility to wash off the posthike sweat. If you wish to camp among the red pines, these are campsites 340–343. Reservations are recommended, as Willow River Campground fills on summer weekends and has one of the highest occupancy rates in the park system. Sites in the 200 campground remain open for winter camping.

Willow Falls, in my opinion, is the most impressive falls in Wisconsin. Back in the 1990s, park personnel removed some dams on the Willow River, freeing the waters to again tumble over this three-tiered drop and produce rumbling echoes between rocky canyon walls. A bridge spans Willow River downstream and offers a great vantage point to view the falls. Willow Falls is accessible only by trail. Footpaths extend beyond the Willow River bridge and climb to the top of the gorge, where more panoramic vistas of the falls below and the land beyond await. More trails in the park crisscross the 3,000 acres through prairies, past an old homestead, and through a surprisingly hilly oak forest. The swim beach on Little Falls

Lake is a big draw during summer. The ultralarge beach has plenty of room to spread out your sunbathing setup on the grass. Picnic tables and a bathhouse complement the area, and canoes and kayaks are available for rent.

The 172-acre Little Falls Lake is a no-gas-or-electric-motors impoundment, which keeps both the lake and the campground serene. Anglers in canoes and rowboats paddle the shoreline of Little Falls Lake for northern pike, largemouth and smallmouth bass, and panfish. Small sailboats are sometimes seen in the impoundment. The Willow River offers good stream fishing for trout. Brown trout, along with a few smallmouth bass, are mostly caught above the Willow Falls. More bass, along with native brook trout, are caught below Little Falls Lake. The park also has a disc golf course and nature center. Check out the naturalist programs, which are offered on summer weekends. Skilled rock climbers tackle walls along the Willow River Gorge.

Nearby attractions include tubing the Apple River and visiting the Twin Cities Mall of America. Contact Float Rite at 715-247-3453 for tubing information. Directions to the Mall of America are at the park entrance station. Proximity to the Twin Cities isn't a bad thing here at Willow River State Park.

Willow River State Park Campground

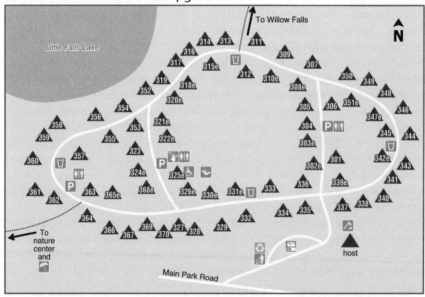

GETTING THERE

From Exit 4 on I-94 near Hudson, take US 12 north 1.8 miles to County Road U. Turn left on CR U and follow it 0.3 mile, and then keep forward on CR A and follow it 1.5 miles to the park, on your left.

GPS COORDINATES: N45° 00.856' W92° 41.486'

NORTHWESTERN WISCONSIN

photographed by RJ and Linda Miller/courtesy of TravelWisconsin.com

Biking the Old Abe State Trail (see page 102)

24

Amnicon Falls State Park Campground

Beauty ★★★ / Privacy ★★★★ / Spaciousness ★★★ / Quiet ★★★★ / Security ★★★★ / Cleanliness ★★★★

The campground here makes for a great layover while you explore the numerous falls at this park.

It is hard to believe how many times I drove past Amnicon Falls without stopping, but one day I decided to see just what this place might have to offer. I'm glad I did. Anyone traveling in northwest Wisconsin should devote a day to setting up camp in this fine campground and visiting the close-by falls in the unhurried manner of someone who knows they are staying for the night. And don't forget to bring your camera as well as your tent.

First established as a Douglas County park in the 1930s, Amnicon Falls grew in size over the years and was eventually taken over by the state in 1961. Since that time, the park has been nicely developed, offering an adequate campground set on a hill. The campground is situated on a single loop, which starts just past the Thimbleberry Nature Trail. Evergreens, such as white spruce and fir, mix with aspens. Younger trees, such as alder and maple, along with underbrush provide decent campsite privacy. Much of the loop's center is grassy and serves as a play area for kids. Most of the campsites are shaded, though some may be open to noonday sun. Campsites 1–6 are first come, first served. The rest of the sites are reservable. The first sites on the outside of the loop are on the edge of the river gorge.

Upper Falls at Amnicon   *photographed by Kevin Revolinski*

KEY INFORMATION

CONTACT: Wisconsin Department of Natural Resources, 715-398-3000, tinyurl.com /amnicon; reservations 888-WI-PARKS, wisconsin.goingtocamp.com

OPEN: Year-round; water available May–October

SITES: 36

EACH SITE: Picnic table, fire ring

ASSIGNMENT: By phone; internet; or first come, first served

REGISTRATION: At entrance station or at campground self-registration station

FACILITIES: Pit toilets, water spigots

PARKING: At campsites and at walk-in parking area

FEE: Wisconsin residents, $18; nonresidents, $23; plus vehicle admission fee (Wisconsin residents, $8; nonresidents, $11; Wisconsin residents age 65 and older, $3); $7.75 reservation fee

ELEVATION: 830'

RESTRICTIONS:

PETS: On leash only

FIRES: In fire ring only; firewood must be purchased in state within 25 miles of campground

ALCOHOL: At campsites only

VEHICLES: 2/site

OTHER: 14-day stay limit

Follow the loop around to reach shady campsite 8. Campsite 11 is well suited for campers with lots of gear, but avoid campsite 14, as it is a bit sloped. Campsites 16 and 17 are two walk-in sites of special note. Campsite 16 is the closest, and campsite 17 is under a big red pine. The campsites beyond here are more open. Campsite 29 works well, and campsites 32 and 33 function as a group site. The river is audible from campsite 35, but the site is very open. Campsite 36 is encircled by brush for privacy seekers.

Amnicon Falls fills only one in three summer weekends. The park is a bit small for extended camping trips, but it's a great spot for a stopover or as part of a tour of the Wisconsin Northwoods.

Waterfall watching is the primary attraction here. There are three main waterfalls at Amnicon: Upper Falls, Lower Falls, and Snake Pit Falls. Numerous other unnamed rapids and cascades show off, too, as the Amnicon River drops 180 feet in its nearly 2-mile jaunt through the park. I was lucky enough to visit the park after a big midsummer rain. The Amnicon was ripping and roaring and flowing strongly. The falls were quite a sight. Visitors admired the beauty and raw power of the water flow that was clearly audible up the hill at the campground. Now and Then Falls, located near Upper Falls, only runs at higher flows; it was pouring a wide veil of water over its ledge that day. Wading and rock-hopping along the river are favorite pastimes here during drier times; only a fool would've gotten in during my stay. The fishing below the falls is fair for muskie, walleye, and northern, and in spring steelhead come upstream from Lake Superior to spawn.

The best way to see the main falls is by a short foot trail that crosses over to an island in midriver. A rustic covered bridge crosses the Amnicon between Upper Falls and Lower Falls. From here, you can listen to the water echoing in the covered bridge. Follow the loop trail around the island perimeter. You have to peer down steeply to see the bottom of Snake Pit Falls. Little side trails spur from the main path as visitors strive to get the best camera angles. Steps have been carved into the rock just above Lower Falls. A short path leads to an open granite outcrop to view Lower Falls. Yet another trail leads up along the Amnicon to view unnamed cascades along the riverbank. The Thimbleberry Nature Trail heads downstream along the Amnicon River to a sandstone quarry, and then loops back along the river escarpment. The accompanying trail booklet will help you learn about this special slice of Wisconsin. I am glad to have learned about Amnicon Falls, especially after passing it by so many times.

Amnicon Falls State Park Campground

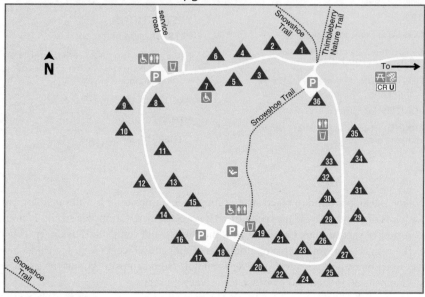

GETTING THERE

From the junction of US 53 and US 2 south of Superior, head east on US 2 for 0.7 mile to County Road U. Turn left on CR U, follow it 0.2 mile, and turn left into the park.

GPS COORDINATES: N46° 36.476' W91° 53.588'

25

Big Bay State Park Campground

Beauty ★★★★ / Privacy ★★★★ / Spaciousness ★★★★ / Quiet ★★★★★ / Security ★★★★★ /
Cleanliness ★★★★★

Big Bay offers you a chance to camp in the famed Apostle Islands.

The biggest of the Apostle Islands chain (and the only one not under the protection of the national lakeshore), Madeline Island is also the only isle inhabited year-round. During the winter, the island boasts a population of about 250; this swells to more than 2,000 in the summer. To reach the island and the 2,500-acre Big Bay State Park, you must pay to take a ferry, but the extra expense and trouble are worth it.

The campground has 60 sites but still exudes a sense of serenity. From Hagen Road, turn left to enter the park, and reach the first of two loops (on the right), which holds campsites 1–30. Here a mixed pine forest reaches overhead, and oaks, maples, spruces, and brush grow beneath the pines. The sites on this loop are generally larger than on the other loop. Campsite 3 is recommended, as it is large and secluded. Campsite 9 is backed against evergreens. Campsites 15 and 21 are good too. A short trail leads from near campsite 22 to Barrier Beach. Campsites 23–25 are large and have good privacy. The end of the loop contains campsites 26–30. These are sizable and are closest to the modern shower building.

Wind and waves cover the rocks with ice formations in winter.

KEY INFORMATION

CONTACT: Wisconsin Department of Natural Resources, 715-747-6425, tinyurl.com /BigBaySP; reservations 888-WI-PARKS, wisconsin.goingtocamp.com

OPEN: Year-round; showers and water available mid-May–first weekend in October

SITES: 38 primitive, 15 electric, 7 walk-in

EACH SITE: Picnic table, fire ring

ASSIGNMENT: By phone; internet; or first come, first served

REGISTRATION: At contact station or self-registration

FACILITIES: Hot showers, flush toilets, vault toilets

PARKING: At campsites and at walk-in parking areas

FEE: Wisconsin residents, $22 ($32 electric site); nonresidents, $27 ($37 electric site); plus vehicle admission fee (Wisconsin residents, $8; nonresidents, $11; Wisconsin residents age 65 and older, $3); $7.75 reservation fee; Madeline Island ferry, one-way: vehicle, $13.50; passengers age 12 and older, $8; passengers ages 6–11, $3.50

ELEVATION: 625'

RESTRICTIONS:

PETS: On 8-foot leash only

FIRES: In fire ring only; firewood must be purchased in state within 25 miles of campground

ALCOHOL: At campsites only

VEHICLES: 2/site

OTHER: 14-day stay limit

The second loop has a real mix of open and shaded campsites. Campsite 33 is well shaded. Tent campers should consider the walk-in campsites 35–41. A gravel path makes a miniloop to reach shady sites beneath spruce, birch, and maple trees. The second road loop continues. The sites on the inside of the loop are more open, whereas the sites on the outside of the loop are shaded and screened by evergreens. The last five campsites have a mix of sun and shade.

All of the 60 campsites are reservable. As summer warms here in the very north of Wisconsin, the campground fills. Sites are hard to come by without reservations anytime in July and August. Be sure to reserve in advance, or consider coming here in early June or September, when last-minute sites are more easily had. Also, watch out for the raccoons here. They can be very pesky. Bears have been known to visit as well.

Campers like to pedal on park roads and around Madeline Island, but bikes are not allowed on the 7 total miles of park trails. The tan sands of Barrier Beach curve along Big Bay and make for excellent photography spots. Many hardy swimmers dip in Lake Superior here. Folks also surf-fish here or at other areas of the park's extensive shoreline for rainbow, lake, and brown trout. The lagoon behind Barrier Beach offers angling for pike. Canoes, paddleboats, and rowboats can be rented at Town Park, which also abuts the lagoon. Other parts of the shore feature craggy sandstone rocks, such as the outcrop at the park picnic area. Waves crash against boulders that have fallen off the cliffs into the water.

Many campers like to hike the trails. Barrier Beach has a boardwalk that offers interpretive information along the shore of Lake Superior. Lagoon Ridge Trail stretches for 2.5 miles through the park's interior and connects to the Bay View Trail, which cruises along the shore for another 1.5 miles. Point Trail also meanders along the edge of the lake.

Indigenous natives had inhabited Madeline Island for thousands of years before Europeans discovered it in the 1660s. Fur traders, missionaries, and fishermen followed. You can learn about the island's culture and life by taking an island bus tour, or check out the Madeline Island Museum in the village of La Pointe, the "town" on the island. La Pointe has stores and restaurants too. You can rent mopeds or bicycles for wheeled explorations of Madeline Island. Various waterborne sightseeing tours of the adjacent Apostle Islands National Lakeshore are available in Bayfield; visit apostleisland.com for more information.

While the campground is open year-round, keep in mind that the ferry operates only from the spring ice breakup, generally late March or early April, to freeze-up, usually in January. For a period of time, Madeline Island is accessible by snow road. If you do come then, campsites 26–30 are kept open. The lake ice and wind-borne spray from the big lake make for a very dramatic and picturesque lakeshore. You will be sure to get a campsite, but remember to bring lots of extra clothes!

Big Bay State Park Campground

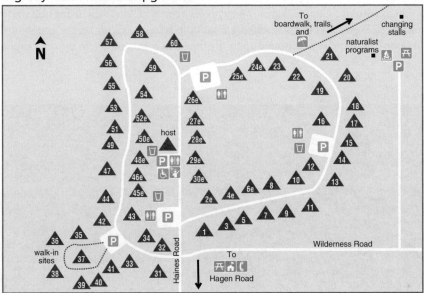

GETTING THERE

From the intersection of US 2 and WI 13 west of Ashland, follow WI 13 north 19.7 miles into Bayfield, until the right turn to the Madeline Island Ferry. After debarking the ferry in La Pointe, veer right, and then turn left on Main Road. Keep forward 6 miles. Main Road turns into Hagen Road at 4 miles; the park will be on the left.

GPS COORDINATES: N46° 47.311' W90° 39.993'

26

Birch Grove Campground

Beauty ★★★★ / Privacy ★★★★★ / Spaciousness ★★★★ / Quiet ★★★★★ / Security ★★★ / Cleanliness ★★★

This campground lies between two small, scenic lakes.

Birch Grove Campground lies on an isthmus of land between two attractive Northwoods lakes. This setup makes for twice the water, twice the fishing, and twice the beauty. The small size of the campground and its setting in a secluded parcel of the Chequamegon-Nicolet National Forest combine for a relaxed ambience perfect for a getaway from the busy side of life. When I got to Birch Grove, the skies were dark and the winds were cool. A few other campers, mostly huddled by campfires, were around. The only sounds to be heard were winds pushing through the birch and aspen trees and birds galore that didn't seem to mind the chill, plus a chattering chipmunk determined to get a handout. Luckily, a hiking trail stretches around West Twin Lake; the other lake is East Twin Lake. I took off on the approximately 1-mile loop trail and was fully heated up by the time that path returned to the campground.

Valhalla Trail

courtesy of the U.S. Forest Service/public domain

KEY INFORMATION

CONTACT: USFS Washburn Ranger District, 715-373-2667, www.fs.usda.gov/cnnf

OPEN: May 6–mid-October

SITES: 16

EACH SITE: Picnic table, fire grate

ASSIGNMENT: First come, first served

REGISTRATION: Self-registration on-site

FACILITIES: Vault toilets, pump wells

PARKING: At campsites only

FEE: $12

ELEVATION: 1,100'

RESTRICTIONS:

PETS: On leash only

FIRES: In fire ring only; firewood must be purchased in state within 25 miles of campground

ALCOHOL: At campsites only

VEHICLES: No restrictions

OTHER: 14-day stay limit

I set up camp at site 13 and made my own fire. Later, the day warmed somewhat, and I fully enjoyed my experience at Birch Grove. Campsite 13 is not the only good site here. Most make for ideal tent sites. Paper birch trees, many of them with multiple trunks, grow abundantly on the land between the lakes. Red maples, red oaks, and spruce trees are common, too, though a 2016 storm knocked many of them down. Heavy vegetation thrives between the campsites. The campground is strung out along a road between the waters and lies a bit closer to West Twin Lake than East Twin Lake. Pass the fee station and come to campsite 1, set on a hill above West Twin Lake. Campsite 2 lies across the gravel road from the boat ramp for East Twin Lake. Campsite 3 is close to East Twin and is heavily shaded. Campsites 5 and 7 are set back a bit from East Twin. After the road veers closer to West Twin Lake, you'll reach campsites 4, 6, and 8, which overlook West Twin and have short trails leading to the water's edge. Reach the first of two pump wells and the short, small ramp leading into West Twin Lake. The shore beside the boat ramp has been stabilized with wood timbers, creating a grassy sitting area next to a tiny beach. Junior could take a dip here or shore-fish, while Mom and Dad watch the action from nearby benches.

Campsite 9 is large and set across from a set of vault toilets. Campsites 11, 12, and 13 lie along West Twin Lake. Reach a turnaround loop that has a pump well in its center. Campsite 14 is at the back of the loop and offers solitude but is less shaded. Campsites 15 and 16 also are isolated but don't offer lake views because they are set a bit back from East Twin Lake.

The hiking trail around West Twin Lake meanders over wooded hills, where bracken ferns reach waist high, and then continues through younger, forested areas and along the shoreline. A short boardwalk leads into a small tamarack bog. The 16-acre West Twin Lake offers decent fishing for northern pike, largemouth bass, and panfish. East Twin Lake is a little bigger at 22 acres and offers the same species as West Twin Lake. Both have completely undeveloped shorelines that make for pleasant watery outings.

A spur trail leads to the 13.5-mile Valhalla Trail, a wilderness loop popular for ATVs. Nearby Long Lake, passed on the way into Birch Grove, is renowned for its crystal-clear water. (East and West Twin Lakes both have clear water too.) At 36 acres, Long Lake has good fishing for largemouth bass. The boat ramp at Long Lake is carry in. The picnic area has a swim beach and is very pretty. If you intend to swim at Long Lake or either of the Twin Lakes, then I hope the weather will be warmer for you than it was for me during my camping trip at Birch Grove.

Birch Grove Campground

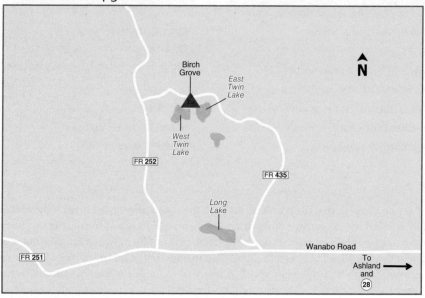

GETTING THERE

From the intersection of US 2 and WI 13 west of Ashland, drive north on WI 13 for 5.6 miles to Wanabo Road. Turn left on Wanabo Road and follow it 6 miles to Forest Road 435. Turn right on FR 435 and follow it 2.8 miles to the campground, on your left.

GPS COORDINATES: N46° 41.066' W91° 3.599'

27

Black Lake Campground

Beauty ★★★★ / Privacy ★★★★★ / Spaciousness ★★★★ / Quiet ★★★★★ / Security ★★★ /
Cleanliness ★★★★

Most of the campsites here are lakefront.

Whoever laid out Black Lake Campground made the most of the lakeside woods. Twenty-one of the 29 campsites abut this attractive lake in the Northwoods, which is completely encircled by national forest property. The arrangement creates an appealing setting to pitch your tent, absorb nature, and maybe enjoy some outdoor recreation. However, a laid-back campground such as this beckons you to snooze in the chair or take a little nap in the hammock as much as hiking down the trail.

Soon after the campground entrance, the lake comes into view just as you reach the Black Lake Picnic Area and the first boat launch. This is also the parking for campsites 27–29, which are walk-in sites reached via the first portion of the Black Creek Trail. The campsite trail spurs right and leads to three top-notch camps beneath towering red pines. Each of these campsites offers a great view of Black Lake and a sense of seclusion unrivaled

The undeveloped shoreline of Black Lake   *courtesy of the U.S. Forest Service/public domain*

KEY INFORMATION

CONTACT: USFS Great Divide Ranger District, 715-634-4821, www.fs.usda.gov/cnnf; reservations 877-444-6777, recreation.gov

OPEN: Mid-May–November

SITES: 29

EACH SITE: Picnic table, fire ring, a few also have upright grill

ASSIGNMENT: By phone; internet; or first come, first served

REGISTRATION: Self-registration on-site

FACILITIES: Vault toilet, pump well

PARKING: At campsites and at walk-in campsite parking

FEE: $12

ELEVATION: 1,400'

RESTRICTIONS:

PETS: On leash only

FIRES: In fire ring only; firewood must be purchased in state within 10 miles of campground

ALCOHOL: At campsites only

VEHICLES: No restrictions

OTHER: 14-day stay limit

even at the rest of this remote campground. These sites are the best at Black Lake, and that is saying quite a lot.

Cross the outflow of Black Lake. This spot beneath a white pine is a favored fishing hole. Enter the main campground road, which is paved, to see a series of widely spaced campsites spur toward the lake. They are cut into woods of paper birch, red pine, and some spruce and aspen trees. Ferns and smaller trees form a thicket-like understory that allows maximum campsite privacy. The campsites away from the lake are even more thickly wooded and private but are used less.

A vault toilet lies past campsite 7. A pump well is next to campsite 13, which is very large. Many other sites are so large that they are open to the sun in the center. The sites become even more widely separated after 13. Campsites 16 and 17 are in a grove of paper birches. Campsite 19 is closest to the water. A short road to the campground boat landing lies beyond 19. The campground ends in a miniloop. The first part of the miniloop has no campsites, and then lakeside sites resume with 20. Campsite 22 is highly recommended.

All sites are reservable. Be advised that the Black Lake Trail runs between the campsites and the lake itself. Two pump wells serve the campground. The bathrooms here are the newer SST models. SST is short for "sweet-smelling technology," an improvement over the hole-in-the-ground technology of old.

Black Lake covers 129 acres, and motorized boats are allowed. Commonly sought fish species include muskellunge, largemouth bass, northern pike, and panfish. A swim beach lies along the lake, midway in the campground. A sloped grassy area dips into the water and leads to a small roped area in the lake.

The 4-mile Black Lake Trail is a highlight of the area. It loops entirely around the lake, crossing Fishtrap Creek via a bridge. Along the way are interpretive stops where you can learn about the logging history of the recovered woods. Pass through an old logging camp-site, along a railroad grade, and by tree plantations from the 1930s. Much of Wisconsin's Northwoods were cut over by the 1930s, after harvesting huge white pines and other trees. The federal government came in and bought these lands from timber companies, private landowners, and counties that had little use for tax-forfeited cutover land. The U.S. Forest Service came in, and young men in the Great Depression–era Civilian Conservation Corps planted thousands of trees. The regenerated forests provide timber for harvest, give food and cover for wildlife, protect watersheds from erosion, and make recreation areas such as Black Lake viable again. Just remember that when you snooze in the shade under that tall tree.

Black Lake Campground

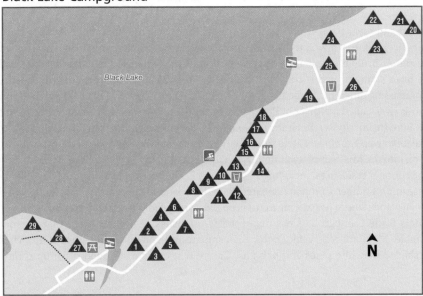

GETTING THERE

From Loretta, drive north on County Road GG for 8 miles to Forest Road 172. Turn left on FR 172 and follow it 5.6 miles. Stay straight 0.1 mile farther, now on FR 173, and then turn right onto paved FR 1666 into the campground.

GPS COORDINATES: N45° 59.276′ W90° 55.794′

28

Bois Brule Campground

Beauty ★★★★ / Privacy ★★★ / Spaciousness ★★★★ / Quiet ★★★★ / Security ★★★★ / Cleanliness ★★★★

Tent camp next to one of Wisconsin's best—and coldest—paddling rivers.

Canoers and kayakers develop a certain reverent tone when they talk about paddling the Bois Brule River. I don't know if it is the history, scenery, trout fishing, rapids, or what, but a trip on the Bois Brule is a near-religious experience for many Badger State floating aficionados. Bois Brule Campground is conveniently located midway along the river, offering float trips encompassing different characters of the river amid the 42,000-acre Brule River State Forest.

This river, called the River of Presidents due to the many American leaders who have cast lines here (from Ulysses S. Grant to Dwight D. Eisenhower), first saw the Chippewa tribe make its way up the chilly waters from Lake Superior, and then portage to the St. Croix River and on into the Mississippi River drainage. Voyageurs and fur traders followed the Chippewa. Later, summer residences, including Cedar Island Estate, were built along the Brule. Still later, Nebagamon Lumber Company donated Bois Brule land to the state, which, along with the riverside landowners, has attempted to keep this spring-fed watershed beautiful.

Bois Brule Campground has many stellar campsites, as well as some that are merely desirable. Most are reservable. Enter the campground and come to campsite 1, a walk-in site shaded by white pines and balsams. Campsite 2 offers a secluded drive-up campsite,

Paddlers on the upper Bois Brule River

photographed by Philip Olson/courtesy of TravelWisconsin.com

KEY INFORMATION

CONTACT: Wisconsin Department of Natural Resources, 715-372-5678, dnr.wi.gov/topic/StateForests/bruleriver; reservations 888-WI-PARKS, wisconsin.goingtocamp.com

OPEN: Year-round; water available May–October

SITES: 20

EACH SITE: Picnic table, fire ring, wood bench

ASSIGNMENT: First come, first served and by reservation

REGISTRATION: Self-registration on-site

FACILITIES: Vault toilets, pump well

PARKING: At sites and walk-in parking area

FEE: Wisconsin residents, $16; nonresidents, $21; plus vehicle admission fee (Wisconsin residents, $8; nonresidents, $11; Wisconsin residents age 65 and older, $3); $7.75 reservation fee

ELEVATION: 1,000'

RESTRICTIONS:

PETS: On 8-foot leash only

FIRES: In fire ring only; firewood must be purchased in state within 10 miles of campground

ALCOHOL: At campsites only

VEHICLES: 2/site

OTHER: One family or 6 unrelated adults/site

while campsites 3–5 rest on a flat shaded by towering red pines. State forest service personnel have planted evergreens that now provide privacy between the sites. The campground road splits, and large boulders keep cars where they should be. The sites along the right road lie on the edge of the escarpment above Bois Brule River. Near this road are three excellent walk-in tent sites, 7–9. Drop down steps to the heavily shaded and wooded river plain. These next three sites stretch along the river and are worth toting gear up and down the steps. I stayed at campsite 10, which has much privacy vegetation. The campground opens up again with sites 11–13 under pines.

The left campground road holds sites 14–19. These sites are generally open under the pines and lack an understory. Most are large, so bring the big tent. The final campsite, 20, sits by itself, offering maximum privacy and shade.

Water can be had at the artesian well by the park headquarters garage, just a bit down Ranger Station Road. Vault toilets are near any site in the campground, which fills nearly every summer weekend. I advise making a special effort and coming during the week, when the campground and river are serene.

Most anyone can paddle the upper 26 miles of the river, which drops at a rate of 3.5 feet per mile, though there are some named rapids. Then comes a stretch of 12 miles dropping at 17 feet per mile, much of it just below Copper Range Campground, including Mays Ledges, which has been known to dump a paddler or two. The last part of the river levels out before reaching Lake Superior. Luckily, Brule River Canoe Rental is located a mere mile from the campground. It offers canoes, kayaks, and shuttle services covering the entire river; call them at 715-372-4983 or visit brulerivercanoerental.com.

Hikers have options here too. Stoney Hill Nature Trail runs 1.7 miles just across from Bois Brule Campground. You can enjoy a view of the landscape from an old fire tower site. Hikers can also travel 16 miles of the North Country Trail here. The Historic Portage Trail in the forest's southwest corner follows the 2-mile portage route connecting the Bois Brule to Upper St. Croix Lake. Many angler parking areas are located along the Brule, especially the lower river. Coldwater species range from trout to salmon. A picnic area is located at the mouth of the Brule, where you can overlook Lake Superior from a bluff, and even take a swim if you dare. A long sandy beach stretches beside the big lake. After your first visit, you may be stretching out your tent-camping adventure in the Brule River State Forest.

Bois Brule Campground

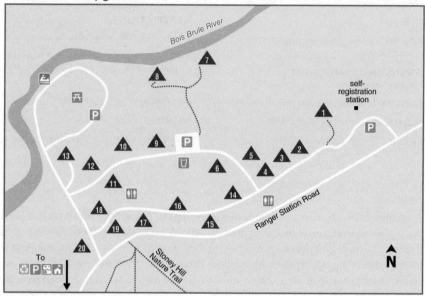

GETTING THERE

From the intersection of US 53 and US 2 south of Superior, drive east on US 2 for 16 miles to the town of Brule. Turn right on Ranger Station Road, just beyond the bridge over the Bois Brule River, and keep forward on Ranger Station Road 1 mile to reach the campground, on your right.

GPS COORDINATES: N46° 32.379' W91° 35.493'

Brunet Island State Park Campground

Beauty ★★★ / Privacy ★★ / Spaciousness ★★★ / Quiet ★★★ / Security ★★★★ / Cleanliness ★★★★

Camp on an island in the Chippewa River.

The Chippewa River is a historic waterway, used for travel by Wisconsin's first peoples long before voyageurs, loggers, and settlers arrived in Chippewa Valley. One fellow, a Frenchman named Jean Brunet, stands out among the later history makers of this region. Brunet came to the United States from France in 1828 and settled in Chippewa Falls, where he established the first sawmill in the area. He later became a state legislator representing Chippewa Falls. But civilized life was too much for Brunet, and he pushed farther up the Chippewa River Valley, settling near this present-day park at a falls on the Chippewa. He operated a ferry and trading post here until he died in 1877. Today, Brunet Island State Park bears his name, and the rustic island exhibits the spirit of this pioneer. Now you can camp here and enjoy even more nonisland land on the banks of the Chippewa River.

There are two campgrounds to choose from, but campers will want to avoid pitching their tents in the South Campground. The 24 sites found there have electrical hookups, making it an RV haven. However, this campground has the only shower building at Brunet Island, so campers may not want to avoid it altogether. The North Campground is much more to a tent camper's liking. Set partly along the Chippewa River and partly along a couple of lagoons off the river, this loop holds campsites 25–69. A hardwood forest mixed with white pines and hemlocks stands overhead, but the very high deer population keeps any understory within easy reach eaten away, obliterating all understory and privacy in the campground. The first set of sites includes 25–43. Campsites on both sides of the road overlook water, with sites on the left-hand side of the loop directly on the Chippewa River. Bridge the outlet of a lagoon and reach the second set of sites between two lagoons of the Chippewa. These sites are more heavily wooded than the first set. A small miniloop at the end has more shaded

Campers gather to socialize at Brunet Island.

photographed by Glenn Sanderson/courtesy of TravelWisconsin.com

KEY INFORMATION

CONTACT: 715-239-6888, dnr.wi.gov/topic /parks/name/brunetisland; reservations 888-WI-PARKS, wisconsin.goingtocamp.com

OPEN: Year-round; water available from last frost of spring to first frost of fall

SITES: 45 primitive, 24 electric

EACH SITE: Picnic table, fire ring

ASSIGNMENT: First come, first served and by reservation

REGISTRATION: At entrance station

FACILITIES: Hot showers, flush toilets, pit toilets, water spigots

PARKING: At campsites only

FEE: Wisconsin residents, $20 ($30 electric site); nonresidents, $25 ($35 electric site); plus vehicle admission fee (Wisconsin residents, $8; nonresidents, $11; Wisconsin residents age 65 and older, $3); $7.75 reservation fee

ELEVATION: 1,025'

RESTRICTIONS:

PETS: On leash only

FIRES: In fire ring only; firewood must be purchased in state within 10 miles of campground

ALCOHOL: At campsites only

VEHICLES: 2/site

OTHER: 21-day stay limit

---

sites. Recommended reservable campsites include 33, 42, 44, 46–48, 52, and 64. Do not take 65, as it is small and flood-prone.

Brunet Island campers are mostly locals and families who live within about a 40-mile radius, so it tends to fill on summer weekends. Reservations are highly recommended. Insects can be bothersome at times. Call ahead for the latest bug update before you make your reservation.

With all this water around, it is no wonder that boating and paddling are popular activities here. Motorboaters are mostly fishermen, as the Chippewa and adjacent Fisher Rivers are too rocky for recreational boating. Anglers can find some good fishing for muskie, walleye, smallmouth bass, and catfish. Spring and fall are good for panfish. Canoes and kayaks can be rented in nearby Cornell. The islands and back bays of the area make for good wildlife watching and fishing spots. The shoreline of the Chippewa River is undeveloped for 3 miles upriver and 1 mile up the Fisher River. The current here is generally moderate, as the Chippewa is dammed not too far downstream. A fishing pier is located near the South Campground and in the lagoon at the center of the North Campground. A large picnic area and swim beach are located on the south end of the island.

Over 7 miles of hiking trails course across Brunet Island and the adjoining mainland. Old-growth hemlock trees tower over the Jean Brunet Nature Trail and along parts of the Timber Trail. The Nordic Trail makes a 2.8-mile loop on the "mainland." Bikers often pedal the paved park roads. A 1-mile paved bike trail connects to the 20-mile Old Abe State Trail. This trail was named for an eagle used in the Civil War as a mascot for troops from Wisconsin. This rail-trail extends south for 20 miles to near Lake Wissota State Park (see page 64).

Brunet Island State Park Campground

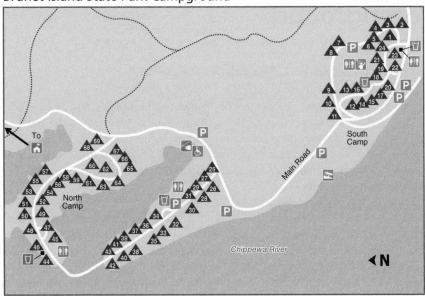

GETTING THERE

From Chippewa Falls, take WI 178 north 21 miles to WI 64. Keep forward on WI 64 east and follow it over the Chippewa River into Cornell, turning left on Park Road after 1 mile. Follow Park Road 1 mile into the park.

GPS COORDINATES: N45° 10.762' W91° 10.335'

30

Copper Falls State Park Campground

Beauty ★★★ / Privacy ★★★★ / Spaciousness ★★★ / Quiet ★★★★ / Security ★★★★ / Cleanliness ★★★★

Three waterfalls are only part of the natural beauty here.

This park's namesake is just one element of the beauty found at this Wisconsin jewel. The Bad River and its feeder branches gain water from lakes and streams to the south. Then they begin cutting through gorgeous scenery, which includes not only Copper Falls but also Brownstone Falls and other cascades and ledges amid craggy, colorful rock formations and thick forests. The camping doesn't quite match the incredible scenery, but it will pass muster for most tent campers.

Copper Falls actually has two camping areas. The better of the two, the South Campground, has sites 34–56. Pass a modern shower building, and then reach the first five-site miniloop. A dense hardwood forest shades these campsites, which are somewhat pinched in, but they do have dense swaths of greenery between them. The second miniloop also has five campsites and backs up against a hill. The third miniloop holds 12 campsites. Pass five shaded sites, and then reach the walk-in sites. A trail leads uphill to a level bench, where

Water cascades along Tyler Forks before it tumbles over Brownstone Falls and joins the Bad River.
courtesy of TravelWisconsin.com

KEY INFORMATION

CONTACT: 715-274-5123, dnr.wi.gov/topic /parks/name/copperfalls; reservations 888-WI-PARKS, wisconsin.goingtocamp.com

OPEN: Year-round

SITES: 43 primitive, 13 electric

EACH SITE: Picnic table, fire grate

ASSIGNMENT: By phone; internet; or first come, first served

REGISTRATION: At campground entrance station

FACILITIES: Hot showers, flush toilets, vault toilets, water spigot

PARKING: At campsites and at walk-in camper parking area

FEE: Wisconsin residents, $22 ($32 electric site); nonresidents, $27 ($37 electric site); plus vehicle admission fee (Wisconsin residents, $8; nonresidents, $11; Wisconsin residents age 65 and older, $3); $7.75 reservation fee

ELEVATION: 1,100'

RESTRICTIONS:

PETS: On leash only

FIRES: In fire ring only; firewood must be purchased in state within 10 miles of campground

ALCOHOL: At campsites only

VEHICLES: 2/site

OTHER: 21-day stay limit

---

these desirable sites are located under hardwoods. A cart aids campers in toting their gear. The last few sites on this loop, 53–56, are larger than the rest in the South Campground.

The North Campground is strung out along a side road. While these sites are a little larger than those in the South Campground, they are more open to overhead sun. Evergreens and small trees screen the average-size campsites from one another. Campsites 1–13 are electric and draw in the hard-sided tents, also known as RVs. The road climbs a bit and splits. The right road leads to campsites 16–29, which are open to the sun overhead too. The left-road sites, 30–33, are more shaded and secluded. Campsite 33 is the most isolated in the entire campground. All but four sites, including all the walk-in sites, are reservable. Definitely make reservations, as this campground can fill daily late June–late August.

Copper Falls is a hiker's park. The best way to see the beauty around here is by foot. The Nature Trail is the primary attraction. It starts at the large and pretty park picnic area. Before you hit the trail, check out the historic and picturesque log building at the trailhead, built by the Civilian Conservation Corps in the 1930s. This building houses a concession stand in the summer. It offers ice cream, cold drinks, and light lunches. Cross a bridge over Bad River just upstream of its entrance into the gorge. To the left, you can climb to an observation tower and gain a perspective on the countryside. The trail to the right leads to Copper Falls and views into the ragged, craggy rocks and frothing water of the gorge. Cross a second bridge to reach the Devils Gate, a rocky area through which the Bad River cuts. Brownstone Falls lies at the mouth of Tyler's Fork River, where it drops into Bad River. The third bridge leads back to the picnic area. The whole gorge is alive with a rich forest that contrasts with the ancient red-brown rock of the gorge, once unsuccessfully mined for copper.

The North Country National Scenic Trail runs directly through the North Campground. Also, on its 5-mile trek through Copper Falls, the North Country Trail descends Bad River Gorge to the north and past Loon Lake to the south. Hikers can also walk the 2.5-mile Red

Granite Falls Trail, which passes yet another scenic waterfall. Hikers can join mountain bikers on two other loops, one of which passes Murphy Lake.

More than 8 miles of river run through the park. Bad and Tyler's Fork Rivers offer challenging fishing for rainbow, brown, and brook trout. Lake anglers can try their hand at Loon Lake, a no-motor venue offering largemouth bass, northern pike, and panfish. If you want to dunk yourself instead of a line, head for the sandy swim beach at Loon Lake. Swimming is prohibited in the Bad River due to the sharp rocks and fast water. However, exploration on the park trails is encouraged at this protected jewel of a park.

Copper Falls State Park Campground

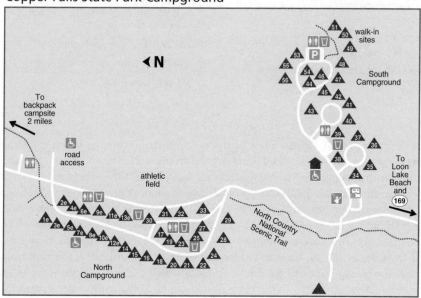

GETTING THERE

From Mellen, head north on WI 13 for 0.5 mile to WI 169. Turn right on WI 169 and follow it 1.6 miles to the park, on your left.

GPS COORDINATES: N46° 21.987' W90° 38.836'

31

Day Lake Campground

Beauty ★★★★★ / Privacy ★★★★★ / Spaciousness ★★★★★ / Quiet ★★★★ / Security ★★★ / Cleanliness ★★★★

Campsite beauty is second only to natural beauty here at Day Lake.

The beautiful 640-acre lake that the campground sits on serves as a haven for wildlife. Waterfowl, especially loons, congregate on the lake's many floating islands. But the first thing you will notice is the very large campground. Under most circumstances, a campground this large would hold twice the number of campsites here at Day Lake, but those responsible for developing the campground gave each site more than ample room. And a myriad of outdoor activities are quite convenient. Boating, fishing, swimming, and hiking are just feet away, so pack your tent, bring your watercraft and fishing pole, and be prepared to have a good time.

Day Lake Campground is broken into six large loops with no more than 10 campsites per loop. Overhead, tall red pines, jack pines, paper birches, and sugar maples sway with gentle breezes. A thick understory of ferns, brush, and small trees such as alders screen campsites from one another. Overall, the sites are as far apart as you are going to see in any drive-up campground. The campground as a whole is neat and well kept. Surprisingly, Day Lake doesn't often fill on weekends. I nabbed a first-come, first-served campsite on July 4! But to eliminate worries, campsites are reservable.

Day Lake beckons on warm summer days.

courtesy of Dave Melancon/U.S. Forest Service, Eastern Region/public domain

KEY INFORMATION

CONTACT: USFS Great Divide Ranger District,
715-264-2511, www.fs.usda.gov/cnnf;
reservations 877-444-6777, recreation.gov

OPEN: May–October

SITES: 52

EACH SITE: Picnic table, fire ring

ASSIGNMENT: By phone; internet;
or first come, first served

REGISTRATION: Self-registration on-site

FACILITIES: Vault toilets, pump wells

PARKING: At campsites only

FEE: $14

ELEVATION: 1,460'

RESTRICTIONS:

PETS: On leash only

FIRES: In fire ring only; firewood must be
purchased in state within 10 miles of
campground

ALCOHOL: At campsites only

VEHICLES: No restrictions

OTHER: 14-day stay limit

Each loop is reached via a spur road leading left from the main road. The first loop, Jack Pine Circle, houses campsites 1–10. Jack pines dominate the tree cover. Campsites 7–9 face Day Lake and are reservable. The next loop, Heron Circle, is set away from the water but offers ample space and privacy. The sites here, 11–17, lie on the outside of the loop and, except for 17, can all be reserved.

The next spur road leads to Paper Birch and Red Pine Circles. Paper Birch is paved and has sites suitable for RVs, few of which ever show up. A couple of the all-access sites have paved pads. Campsites 18–22 are toward the lake. Some of the sites are so large that they are open to the noon sun overhead. The Red Pine Circle has even larger sites at 29–39. Try reserving sites 29 or 30 if you want a lot of room.

The Blueberry Circle has only six campsites, 40–45. All are first come, first served and are the least used in the entire campground. The loop is a bit away from the lake, but the sites are all desirable. The potentially buggy brush and tree marsh lying near campsites 41 and 42 must scare campers away. However, campsite 42 offers the most solitude in the entire campground. Musky Bay Circle, with sites 46–52, is the final loop. It may have the most widely dispersed sites of them all. Campsites 48–49 are toward the lake and are reservable. Each loop has a bathroom and pump wells conveniently located in the center and connected by woodsy paths to the loops.

Day Lake was formed in 1968, when the West Fork of the Chippewa River was dammed. The impoundment created many islands. If you notice some of these islands moving, you aren't seeing things. These masses of vegetation with the occasional small tree are drifting bogs; they provide ideal nesting habitats for loons, which are frequently seen and heard on Day Lake. Muskellunge, largemouth bass, and panfish lie beneath the waters.

Side trails connect the campground to several minipiers for fishing or docking your boat, and an interpretive nature trail runs along the lake, connecting the campground to a picnic area near the dam. Informal shore-fishing spots have been established just off the nature trail. A longer L-shaped fishing pier lies near the Paper Birch Circle.

Kids will enjoy the large, grassy play area near Jack Pine Circle. Here, kids can play on the playground or throw horseshoes while their parents sit on nearby benches. If a swim is desired, there is also a campground swim beach nearby. A sandy waterfront near the picnic area leads to a second roped-off swim beach, where visitors will find yet another fishing pier. Check out the little island by the Day Lake Dam, connected to the mainland by a small wood bridge. Supplies can be had at the small store in nearby Clam Lake. The hamlet also has a few eateries. Get all the food and supplies you want—with these large campsites, you will have plenty of room.

Day Lake Campground

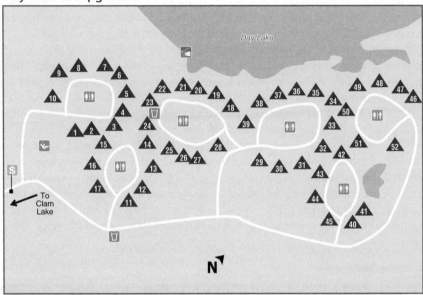

GETTING THERE

From Clam Lake, head west on County Road M 100 yards, and then turn right (north) on CR GG. Keep forward on CR GG 0.8 mile to the campground, on your left.

GPS COORDINATES: N46° 10.905' W90° 54.251'

32

⚲ Lake of the Pines Campground

Beauty ★★★★ / Privacy ★★★ / Spaciousness ★★★ / Quiet ★★★★ / Security ★★★ / Cleanliness ★★★★

This campground lies near the Flambeau River, one of the state's wildest canoeing destinations.

The Flambeau River is a remote watercourse flowing through a state forest of 90,000 acres, where bears, wolves, and other wildlife abound. I found proof of this on the nature trail at Lake of the Pines Campground—fresh bear scat! Don't think that deterred me from staying here overnight. Quite the contrary—it only reinforced my opinion that this was a great place to camp; you are really getting back to nature when a bear or two has enough room to roam. And Lake of the Pines is an ideally located base camp for canoeing both forks of the Flambeau, in addition to other forest pursuits.

Lake of the Pines is the headwater of Connors Creek, which flows into the North Fork Flambeau River. Lake of the Pines Road dead-ends into the campground, which has two loops. The lower loop has eight campsites resting beneath a hardwood forest of sugar maple, birch, basswood, and a few spruce trees. Thick brush grows between most of these widespread sites, all located on the outside of the loop. The road climbs a small hill to the upper loop. These sites are well shaded but are closer together than the lower loop, offering only average campsite privacy. The forested setting is just as pretty as the lower loop. The sites outside the loop are on the edge of a slope that drops off to Lake of the Pines. The loop

Canoeing the Flambeau River

photographed by RJ and Linda Miller/courtesy of TravelWisconsin.com

KEY INFORMATION

CONTACT: Wisconsin Department of Natural Resources, 715-332-5271, dnr.wi.gov/topic/stateforests/flambeauriver; reservations 888-WI-PARKS, wisconsin.goingtocamp.com

OPEN: Year-round

SITES: 30

EACH SITE: Picnic table, fire ring, log bench

ASSIGNMENT: First come, first served

REGISTRATION: Self-registration on-site

FACILITIES: Vault toilets, pump well

PARKING: At campsites only

FEE: Wisconsin residents, $16; nonresidents, $21; plus vehicle admission fee (Wisconsin residents, $8; nonresidents, $11; Wisconsin residents age 65 and older, $3); $7.75 reservation fee

ELEVATION: 1,425′

RESTRICTIONS:

PETS: On leash only

FIRES: In fire ring only; firewood must be purchased in state within 10 miles of campground

ALCOHOL: At campsites only

VEHICLES: 2/site

OTHER: 21-day stay limit

swings away from the water and passes larger sites. These sites back up to a thick forest that makes for an attractive setting. A pump well and vault toilets are provided for each loop. Because this campground fills only on holiday weekends, most sites will be readily available on your average summer weekend.

Paddling is the number-one draw to Flambeau River State Forest. More than 60 miles of water can be canoed or kayaked on the South and North Forks of the Flambeau River. State forestland protects its banks and offers a truly wild setting. Boat landings are adequately spaced along the rivers. The South Fork is rougher and can be too low to run in summer. However, when spring comes, get ready for some good class II–III rapids. You may want to consider portaging around Little Falls Rapid, a class V challenge.

The North Fork is more commonly paddled and has more reliable water. Its uppermost run extends for 12 miles from Nine Mile Creek to Oxbo Landing. The next day trip heads from Oxbo Landing to County Road W, where the forest headquarters is located. This is considered some of the wildest river in the forest, yet it offers fairly gentle water with no named rapids. The next trip, from CR W to Camp Road 41, has the Porcupine Rapids, a three-pitched shoal. The action picks up below Camp Road 41 with two sets of rapids just before the confluence of the South and North Forks. Six more named rapids can be found along the Flambeau before it exits into Big Falls Flowage in Rusk County.

Most paddlers bring a fishing pole to angle for the muskie, walleye, and smallmouth bass that roam the waters. For a more convenient experience, try Lake of the Pines. A boat landing is conveniently located at the campground. Lake of the Pines is noted for its walleye, bass, pike, and crappie fishing. Bass Lake is close if you want a wilderness fishing experience. No motors are allowed, and accessing the lake requires a 0.4-mile boat carry. Try for largemouth bass and bluegill there.

A small swim beach is located on Lake of the Pines via a short path between campsites 13 and 14 on the upper loop. This neat little hideaway offers a grassy shore and small buoys in the water. If you are looking for something bigger, head just a short distance to Connors Lake Picnic Area. It has more than 300 feet of beachfront, complemented with picnic tables, shade trees, and a shelter.

Landlubbers will want to check out the Flambeau Hills Trail System, very near Lake of the Pines. Hikers and bicyclers are welcome to use the 14 miles of interconnected paths that double as winter ski trails. And don't forget the nature trail that loops out of the campground. You might also keep an ear out for one of the wolf packs that roam Flambeau River State Forest.

Lake of the Pines Campground

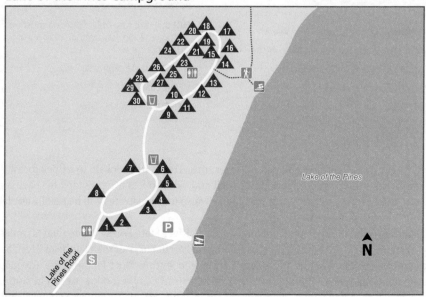

GETTING THERE

From the junction with US 8 in Hawkins, take County Road M north 18 miles to CR W. Turn left on CR W and follow it 1 mile to Lake of the Pines Road. Turn right on Lake of the Pines Road and follow it 1.6 miles to dead-end into the campground.

GPS COORDINATES: N45° 47.058' W90° 42.765'

Lake Three and Beaver Lake Campgrounds

Beauty ★★★★ / Privacy ★★★★ / Spaciousness ★★★ / Quiet ★★★★★ / Security ★★★ / Cleanliness ★★★★

Both of these campgrounds lie in the shadow of St. Peters Dome.

After hearing about the view from St. Peter's Dome, I knew it was a Wisconsin must-see. But where to stay? The two nearby campgrounds, Lake Three and Beaver Lake, both deserved to be included in this guide, but because they were so close to one another, I have lumped them together here. Both offer small, secluded, and quiet campgrounds and great lakeside tent camping. And there are plenty of hiking, boating, and fishing opportunities nearby.

St. Peter's Dome
courtesy of the U.S. Forest Service/public domain

The 10 campsites at Beaver Lake are strung out on a small loop beside the water. All can be reserved. A forest of maples, basswoods, aspens, birches, and evergreens shades this campground and provides mostly good campsite privacy. The first three campsites lie away from the lake but near the pump well and vault toilet. Campsite 2 is a small, tent-only unit. The loop curves around past a marshy downhill and below the camp to reach campsite 4. This large and attractive site overlooks Beaver Lake. Campsites 5, 7, and 8 all have good lake views with short water-access trails. Campsite 7 has the best lake view of them all. Campsites 6, 9, and 10 are inside the loop.

Lake Three Campground has eight sites, all first come, first served. Campsite 1 is inside the loop but is well screened with spruce and fir trees. Maples tower overhead. Campsite 2 is large and set away from the road. Campsite 3 may be the best of all; it is large and closest to the lake. Continuing on, you'll reach an area of shaded but open campsites. Farther along the loop is campsite 4; located inside the loop, this small site is shaded and has open ground. Campsites 5 and 7 are close to the lake but have little privacy. Campsites 6 and 8 are large but are also limited on privacy. The campground pump well is down near the boat landing, which doubles as a swim area. The vault toilet is in the campground loop.

Short access trails from each campground connect to the North Country Trail, which links the two campgrounds. The access trail at Lake Three also leads down to the lake dam, where campers often tie up their boats. West of Beaver Lake is the Marengo Nonmotorized Area, through which the North Country Trail also runs. The Brunsweiler River, a potential trout stream, is 2 miles east from Lake Three on the North Country Trail.

St. Peter's Dome is a mandatory destination for hikers. I hit the trail in the cool of the morning, first stopping at Morgan Falls, a 60-foot narrow cascade slicing between ancient

KEY INFORMATION

CONTACT: USFS Great Divide Ranger District, 715-264-2511, www.fs.usda.gov/cnnf; reservations 877-444-6777, recreation.gov

OPEN: May–October

SITES: Lake Three, 8; Beaver Lake, 10

EACH SITE: Picnic table, fire ring

ASSIGNMENT: By phone; internet; or first come, first served

REGISTRATION: Self-registration on-site

FACILITIES: Vault toilets, pump well

PARKING: At campsites only

FEE: $12

ELEVATION: 1,415'

RESTRICTIONS:

PETS: On leash only

FIRES: In fire ring only; firewood must be purchased in state within 10 miles of campground

ALCOHOL: At campsites only

VEHICLES: No restrictions

OTHER: 14-day stay limit

---

rocks. The path then leads past an old homesite—the rock chimney and well are still discernible. A few ups and downs lead to the final climb, and the northbound view opens before me. From the rock bluff, Morgan Creek and the forest lie in the foreground. Scattered farms with their telltale silos are in the distance. And to the right, 20 miles away, are the waters of Lake Superior. The view is well worth the 2-mile hike to the top. To reach the dome, continue north on Forest Road 187 past Lake Three Campground. After 0.5 mile, turn left on FR 199 and stay with it 5.5 miles to reach the signed trailhead on your right.

Lakes are directly beside both campgrounds. Beaver Lake—35 acres in size—sports trout, panfish, and catfish. A boat landing is 0.5 mile from the campground. Lake Three is 72 acres in size and holds largemouth bass and panfish. The boat ramp here is just off the campground road. A short trail leads to the grassy dam area on Lake Three, and it's a fun place for kids to toss in a line for panfish or watch the bats come out at night from a bat box on the dam levee.

Picking a campground in the shadow of St. Peter's Dome is a tough choice. Neither is bound to fill, except on holiday weekends. You could just take the hike to the top of the dome, and then flip a coin. Either way, you will come out a winner.

GETTING THERE

From the junction with WI 13 in Mellen, drive west on County Road GG 8 miles to Forest Road 187. Turn right on FR 187 (Mineral Lake Road) and follow it 3 miles to Pine Stump Corner. To reach Beaver Lake, keep straight, now on FR 198 for 2 miles, and it will be on the right. To reach Lake Three, turn right at Pine Stump Corner and follow FR 187 for 1 mile, and it will be on the right.

GPS COORDINATES:
BEAVER LAKE N46° 18.107' W90° 53.824'
LAKE THREE N46° 19.083' W90° 51.382'

Lake Three Campground

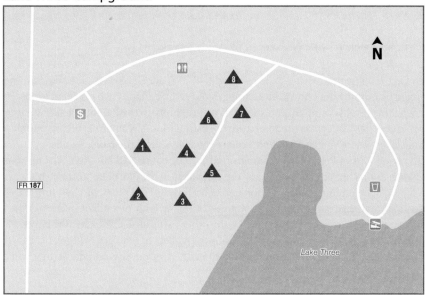

Beaver Lake Campground

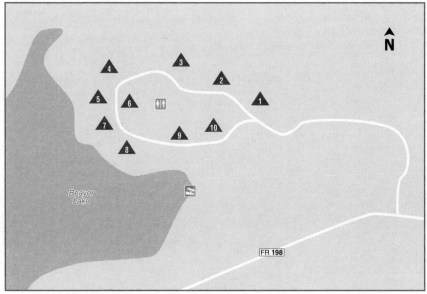

34

Perch Lake Campground

Beauty ★★★★ / Privacy ★★★★ / Spaciousness ★★★★ / Quiet ★★★ / Security ★★★ /Cleanliness ★★★

Explore the Rainbow Lake Wilderness from this campground.

Perch Lake is a fine destination in its own right. The 70-acre lake is scenic and quiet, and it's encircled by nothing but nature. The campground is divided into two excellent loops. However, what makes this campground special is its proximity to the Rainbow Lake Wilderness. This preserve lies just across the road from the campground. Numerous hiking trails lead to pristine lakes where you can fish and explore the wild side of the Northwoods.

The two loops of Perch Lake Campground are not connected but are near one another. The North Loop contains sites 1–10. All the campsites in the North Loop are near the water. Pass the small boat ramp and fee station to reach a forest of red pines, birches, firs, and some white pines that shades the campsites. Campsite 1 is up a bit of a hill; it overlooks the lake and is just steps away from the water, like the other campsites. Campsite 3 is larger. Pass a pump well, and then come to shady campsite 4. Thickets of younger evergreens, as well as distance, screen the campsites from one another. The tree cover is less dense toward Perch

Fishing is popular on Perch Lake.

courtesy of Dave Melancon/U.S. Forest Service, Eastern Region/public domain

KEY INFORMATION

CONTACT: USFS Washburn Ranger District,
715-373-2667, www.fs.usda.gov/cnnf

OPEN: May–October

SITES: 21

EACH SITE: Picnic table, fire grate

ASSIGNMENT: First come, first served

REGISTRATION: Self-registration on-site

FACILITIES: Vault toilets, pump well

PARKING: At campsites only

FEE: $12

ELEVATION: 1,240'

RESTRICTIONS:

PETS: On leash only

FIRES: In fire ring only; firewood must be
purchased in state within 10 miles of
campground

ALCOHOL: At campsites only

VEHICLES: No restrictions

OTHER: 14-day stay limit

Lake, allowing water views. Campsite 8 is very large, yet is close to the water. The road curves away from the water a bit as you approach campsite 9, which is also large. Campsite 10 is farthest from the water and the other campsites. A trail leads from this camp to the lake.

The South Loop holds campsites 11–21 and is set in a hardwood forest with lush grass, ferns, and small trees underneath the maples, oaks, and birches. Enter this lesser-used loop and arrive at the small campsite 19. Like most of the campsites here, it is well shaded. Swing around the loop and pass sites 20 and 21. They are small but secluded. Campsites 17 and 18 are near the fee station and are a bit larger, but they're also very shaded, with moss near the picnic tables. Campsites 11–16 are the largest in the loop and are used more often. They are up a bit of a hill and have many oaks and some pines. Perch Lake is visible below the hill. Campsites 15 and 16 are closest to the lake and are the most popular. Each loop has a pump well and vault toilets. The North Loop is better, but in case it is full, sites on the South Loop should be available in this first-come, first-served campground.

Perch Lake is more than 70 acres in size. Most anglers paddle a canoe or kayak or row a small boat around the water in search of largemouth bass, panfish, and trout. The deepest part of Perch Lake is more than 70 feet down. It averages 19 feet deep, which keeps the water cool enough for trout. Numerous other lakes with small-boat access are just a short drive from Perch Lake. Most notable is Star Lake, a 234-acre no-motor lake. Star Lake has good fishing for muskie, largemouth bass, and panfish. Consult your national forest map to access these other lakes.

Have you ever wanted to hike to a pristine lake in the remote North Country to cast a line, admire the scenery, or simply listen to the sounds of nature? Visit the Rainbow Lake Wilderness, which is 6,600 acres in size. A 6-mile section of the North Country National Scenic Trail crosses the wilderness. Forest Trail 502 leaves from across the South Loop of Perch Lake Campground and heads west to intersect the North Country Trail. Along the way it passes Clay Lake, a 31-acre lake with largemouth bass and panfish. Bufo Lake lies near the junction of the North Country Trail and Forest Trail 502. A scenic lake of 21 acres, Bufo also has largemouth bass and panfish. Beaver Lake is a short walk from a trail access just a bit up Forest Road 35. It offers trout fishing. The other lakes and ponds are also good trout-fishing venues. Here at Perch Lake, you will be able to access water and its recreational opportunities from the campground, from your car, or by foot.

Perch Lake Campground

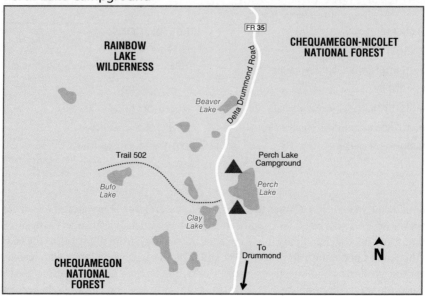

GETTING THERE

From the junction of US 63 and Delta Drummond Road (Forest Road 35), just west of Drummond, drive north on FR 35 for 5.5 miles to the campground, on your right.

GPS COORDINATES: N46° 24.244' W91° 16.238'

35

Spearhead Point Campground

Beauty ★★★★ / Privacy ★★★★ / Spaciousness ★★★ / Quiet ★★★ / Security ★★★★ / Cleanliness ★★★★

Thirteen of the campsites here have their own individual minipiers.

This campground is situated on appropriately named Spearhead Point, a narrow peninsula jutting into 411-acre Mondeaux Flowage, itself a scenic impoundment of the Mondeaux River in Taylor County. This narrow slice of land allows the campground to be nearly surrounded by water, making it a popular campground for boaters, anglers, and water lovers. The added minipiers at most of the campsites make it even more attractive. More than water makes this campground appealing. The blufftop forest shades and screens campsites that look over Mondeaux Flowage. Furthermore, the whole Mondeaux Flowage Recreation Area offers fishing, swimming, and hiking opportunities.

You may just want to hang around this campground. The problem is that eventually you will be drawn to the water, especially if you have a pier extending from your campsite to the lake. Here's the deal: campsites 1, 3, 4, 7, 8, and 11–18 all have these piers. A spur trail leads from the above sites down steps to the water's edge, where a small floating dock makes for easy water access and individual boat docking. You do pay extra for the campsites with piers, as they are designated premium sites, and they tend to go first. However, all campsites in the 1–15 range are reservable, whether they are premium spots or not.

A campsite overlooking Mondeaux Flowage

courtesy of the U.S. Forest Service/public domain

KEY INFORMATION

CONTACT: USFS Medford–Park Falls Ranger District, 715-748-4875, www.fs.usda.gov /cnnf; reservations 877-444-6777, recreation.gov

OPEN: May–October

SITES: 27

EACH SITE: Picnic table, fire ring; some have small dock

ASSIGNMENT: By phone; internet; or first come, first served

REGISTRATION: Self-registration on-site

FACILITIES: Vault toilets, pump well

PARKING: At campsites only

FEE: $12; $14 lakeside sites

ELEVATION: 1,400'

RESTRICTIONS:

PETS: On leash only

FIRES: In fire ring only; firewood must be purchased in state within 10 miles of campground

ALCOHOL: At campsites only

VEHICLES: No restrictions

OTHER: 14-day stay limit

A thick hardwood forest of sugar maples, birches, and basswoods, complemented with a few evergreens, grows on Spearhead Point. Pass the Ice Age Trail, which circles the northern half of Mondeaux Flowage, and reach campsites 25–27, located on the "shaft" of the spearhead. These are among the largest of the campsites here, which are average-size overall. Enter the main campground loop. Smaller spur loops to the right lead to several premium sites, which stand a good 30 feet or more above the water. Campsite 4 is out on the edge of the peninsula. Campsite 8 is very well screened. Pass an attractive shelter building handy for rainy days, as it was during my visit.

Reach another spur loop toward the end of the spearhead containing sites 11–15; here you'll find nothing but lakeside premium sites. Campsite 14 is a little too open. Return to the main loop and pass sites 16–18; all three widely separated campsites are premium sites. Beyond a side road leading to the campground boat landing are four standard campsites that are nice but lack their own piers.

Most campers come here for the water activities. And why not, with the abundance of water access? Mondeaux Flowage offers fishing for muskie, pike, largemouth bass, crappie, and panfish. You can fish from your pier, too, but most folks take their boats out on the lake, dammed back in the 1930s by the Civilian Conservation Corps. An alluring swim beach is located at the Mondeaux Picnic Area. A grassy field borders the buoyed swim area. Picnic tables and a playground complement the beach, as does a snack bar with food, beverages, and ice.

Hikers can enjoy the Ice Age Trail as it follows the northern half of Mondeaux Flowage on its 42-mile trek through the Medford District of the Chequamegon-Nicolet National Forest. A quick hike on the Ice Age Trail could lead from the Mondeaux Picnic Area back to Spearhead Point Campground. The Aldo Leopold Commemorative Trail makes a 1.2-mile loop just across from the Mondeaux Picnic Area. This path, memorializing one of Wisconsin's great naturalists, offers a vista. Another trail of interest is the Chippewa Lobe Interpretive Trail, located west of Mondeaux Flowage. This 7-mile interpretive loop path spurs off the Ice Age Trail, passing interesting glacial features in a primitive no-motor area. To reach this path, drive south from the campground on Forest Road 106, then head west on FR 102, and then south on FR 108. The Ice Age Trail crosses FR 108 and soon offers access to the Chippewa Lobe Interpretive Trail. Chances are, however, that with all the water around you at Spearhead Point, you won't be spending much time on the land.

Spearhead Point Campground

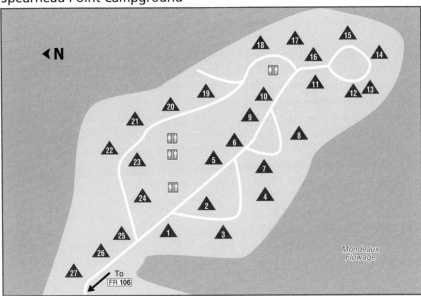

GETTING THERE

From WI 64/13 in Medford, drive north on WI 13 for 15.5 miles to County Road D. Turn left on CR D and follow it 6.5 miles to Forest Road 104. Turn left on FR 104 and follow it 1.1 miles to FR 106. Keep on FR 106 for 1.6 miles to reach the campground, on your left.

GPS COORDINATES: N45° 19.653' W90° 26.693'

36

⛺ St. Croix Campground

Beauty ★★★★★ / Privacy ★★★★★ / Spaciousness ★★★★★ / Quiet ★★★ / Security ★★★ / Cleanliness ★★★★★

Despite its abundance of natural resources, St. Croix Campground is surprisingly underused.

It is hard to believe that a campground this nice and near to so many natural resources is so little used. Set in Governor Knowles State Forest adjacent to the St. Croix Wild and Scenic River, this campground offers first-rate paddling and hiking from a campground that most would love to have as their backyard. I stayed here on a weekday after an overnight canoe trip on the St. Croix River and had the whole campground to myself—in July! St. Croix Campground could also serve as a pretrip stopover spot or as a base camp for day trips on the St. Croix. However, Governor Knowles State Forest stands tall as a destination in its own right, with more than 50 miles of hiking trails, wildlife viewing, and fishing opportunities. This forest parallels the St. Croix River for 55 miles yet never exceeds 2 miles in width. It has an important role in protecting the St. Croix watershed.

St. Croix Campground at Governor Knowles State Forest was developed back in 2000. State forest personnel did a fine job in laying it out. The park road climbs onto an escarpment above the confluence of the Wood River and the St. Croix River. This high-ground location cuts down on insects more prevalent along the banks of the St. Croix. The campground's

Kayakers on the St. Croix River

photographed by Glenn Sanderson/courtesy of TravelWisconsin.com

KEY INFORMATION

CONTACT: Wisconsin Department of Natural Resources, 715-463-2898, dnr.wi.gov /topic/stateforests/govknowles; reservations 888-WI-PARKS, wisconsin.goingtocamp.com

OPEN: First Friday of May–October 15

SITES: 31

EACH SITE: Picnic table, fire ring

ASSIGNMENT: By phone; internet; or first come, first served

REGISTRATION: Self-registration on-site

FACILITIES: Vault toilets, water spigots

PARKING: At campsites only

FEE: Wisconsin residents, $16; nonresidents, $21; $10 extra for electric sites; plus vehicle admission fee (Wisconsin residents, $8; nonresidents, $11; Wisconsin residents age 65 and older, $3); $7.75 reservation fee. Sites 115–119 and 129–130 have electric hookups and get quickly taken by RVs. The host occupies 131 in season.

ELEVATION: 840'

RESTRICTIONS:

PETS: On leash only

FIRES: In fire ring only; firewood must be purchased in state within 10 miles of campground

ALCOHOL: At campsites only

VEHICLES: No restrictions

OTHER: 21-day stay limit

beautiful forest setting is immediately evident. Overhead are tall oaks and white pines, complemented by ash, maple, jack pine, and a few aspen trees. A thick understory of ferns and smaller trees enhances the scene.

The paved campground road leads past widely dispersed campsites that are quite large. Eleven of the 30 sites are on the inside of the loop. Campsite 101 exemplifies the average campground site here: a wide grassy area around a gravel auto pad encircled by tall trees, yet open to noon sun overhead due to its large size. It is surprisingly far to the next campsite.

Drop down a bit of a hill and come to more lush sites bordered with ramparts of ferns. Some of these campsites have wooden benches in front of fire rings cut into the hillside. Climb a bit and come to drier sites. Jack pines and white pines become more prevalent. Just after campsite 114, the Wood River Interpretive Trail leaves right and returns after site 120. The already well-separated sites spread apart even farther after site 124. Three water spigots serve this campground, and there are open sites on weekends (including holiday weekends). Modern vault toilets are accessed via six short trails leading into the loop.

Paddling the St. Croix River is the primary activity around these parts. The river deserves its wild and scenic status. Lush banks of grass and thick trees line the clear water teeming with smallmouth bass and other fish. Slender islands break up the shallow sandy river bottom. The swift current speeds up even more on the occasional riffles and shoals. The wildlife along this river will amaze. I've seen bald eagles, ospreys, a porcupine, ducks, and more deer than people. A canoe landing is located within walking distance of the campground. A short trip would be 5 miles from the campground canoe landing to Stevens Creek Landing, located on the Minnesota side of the river. It is 9 miles down to County O Landing in Wisconsin. Upstream trips can end at the campground landing. Consider putting in a whole day to make the 13-mile float from Nelson's Landing to the campground. This section has many riffles and shoals. Before you come, be sure to visit the St. Croix National Scenic Riverway website at nps.gov/sacn and learn more about potential float trips. Numerous outfitters operate along the river; however, Wild River Outfitters is conveniently located near St. Croix Campground. It offers all lengths of trips and shuttles. For more information, visit wildriverpaddling.com.

Don't forget about hiking here at Governor Knowles State Forest and vicinity. The Wood River Interpretive Trail offers a 1-mile leg stretcher with views of the Wood River and information about the flora and fauna of the area. A spur trail connects the campground with the forest picnic area. Two long trails extend through the forest, each running about 22 miles; these are popular with backpackers. Just north of the campground, at WI 70 landing, is the Sand Rock Cliffs Trail, which makes a narrow 5-mile loop along the St. Croix River and the escarpment above it. The St. Croix Trail extends in both directions from the Marshland Visitor Center just across WI 70 in Minnesota. And after a night or two at St. Croix Campground, you may decide to extend your stay in this underutilized Wisconsin resource.

St. Croix Campground

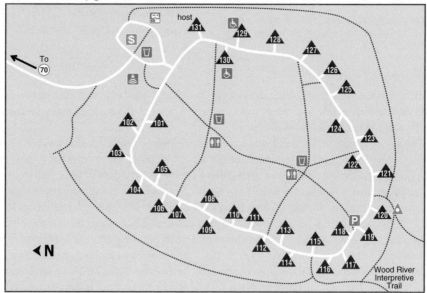

GETTING THERE

From Grantsburg, drive west on WI 70 for 4.5 miles to a left turn into a marked road wayside. Turn left again into the campground.

GPS COORDINATES: N45° 45.837' W92° 46.935'

NORTHEASTERN WISCONSIN

Check out the network of trails at Round Lake Nonmotorized Area (see page 165).

37

⚑ Bagley Rapids Campground

Beauty ★★★★ / Privacy ★★★ / Spaciousness ★★★ / Quiet ★★★★ / Security ★★★ / Cleanliness ★★★

The scenic North Branch Oconto River is just steps away from this campground.

If you look at a map of the Chequamegon-Nicolet National Forest, you will see many private inholdings, denoted in white, amid the holdings owned by the U.S. Forest Service, shaded in green. While scouring campgrounds in Wisconsin, I was certainly glad that the Bagley Rapids Campground along the North Branch Oconto River was "in the green." This destination at the southern end of the Nicolet lies on the North Branch of the Oconto River, a scenic watercourse that originates in lake-studded lands around the hamlet of Wabeno. From Wabeno, the North Branch of the Oconto twists, turns, and falls southward, pausing repeatedly to drop over granite rocks. In other places, the river becomes blocked by fallen timber, forming dark hideaways for the trout that lurk in its waters.

Bagley Rapids Campground is located in what many consider the most impressive stretch of this river. The ledge-type rapids crash and boil over a rocky rampart that provides symphonic music for campers who choose to pitch a tent nearby. And you are very likely to get a site here—the campground is large enough such that all the sites aren't constantly

Sites at Bagley Rapids are especially attractive in the fall.

courtesy of the U.S. Forest Service/public domain

KEY INFORMATION

CONTACT: USFS Lakewood-Laona Ranger District, 715-276-6333, www.fs.usda.gov/cnnf

OPEN: May–October

SITES: 30

EACH SITE: Picnic table, fire grate

ASSIGNMENT: First come, first served

REGISTRATION: Self-registration on-site

FACILITIES: Vault toilet, pump well

PARKING: At campsites only

FEE: $12

ELEVATION: 900'

RESTRICTIONS:

PETS: On leash only

FIRES: In fire ring only; firewood must be purchased in state within 10 miles of campground

ALCOHOL: At campsites only

VEHICLES: 3/site

OTHER: 14-day stay limit

taken, but it's not so big that you feel like you are in a tent suburb. First come, first served means take your chances, but apart from the summer holidays, you should be able to get a campsite at 6 p.m. on Friday, if not noon on Saturday, even during high summer.

To reach the campground, drive through a leafy green cathedral. Overhead is a mix of Northwoods trees, as well as species more comfortable in southern climates. One spot will have dark hemlocks, spruces, or firs; another will have hickories and oaks; and still another will reveal aspens, white pines, or paper birches. The campground has two loops stretched along the noisy river. Strategically placed boulders keep cars parked in their spurs and add a rocky touch to each campsite. Metal campsite fire rings have been placed atop circular rock platforms. Vegetation is thick between the campsites. Trees growing in the middle of the camps keep shady sites even shadier. Fourteen of the 30 sites rest along the river. These sites are the first to go, while the sites on the back of the loop offer more privacy. A little trail reaches the water from nearly every waterside site. Wherever you lay your head, the North Branch Oconto is loud enough to resonate throughout the campground.

Anglers have developed an informal trail system that stretches along the banks of the river and into the campsites. Though these trails travel along the main shoreline, the North Branch of the Oconto defies simple bank-fishing. Here and there, the Oconto splits around islands, creating tougher access for anglers. Casual fishermen won't likely bother with waders and such, but if you really want to fish this river, bring your gripping fishing shoes anytime of year and waders during spring. Otherwise, you can admire the scenery from the shore, or just take a little dip in the pools between fast-moving river rapids.

Just south of Bagley Rapids, the North Branch of the Oconto River flows into Chute Pond, a 417-acre impoundment. This island-dotted lake has muskie, pike, walleye, largemouth bass, and panfish in its waters. A boat ramp is conveniently located south of Bagley Rapids. Skilled paddlers will be seen zipping down the North Fork in spring or at times of higher water. The most popular trip, a 9-mile run, starts on Forest Road 2104 above Mountain. Most rapids are class II. Loon Rapids is 2.4 miles downriver, and then paddlers pass the Old Krammer Dam site, where big boulders lie in the North Branch of the Oconto. The last 2 miles are placid before reaching Bagley Rapids, which are often too rocky to be run, except at high water. End at the campground or take out at the Chute Pond boat ramp. This river run adds fishing possibilities for rainbow, brown, and brook trout. Also, U.S. Forest

Service roads and other roads cross the Oconto and offer fishing access points. Consult a U.S. Forest Service map, which should be ordered before arrival. Supplies can be had back in Mountain or just a bit north in Lakewood. Then you can head back to Bagley Rapids and be "in the green."

Bagley Rapids Campground

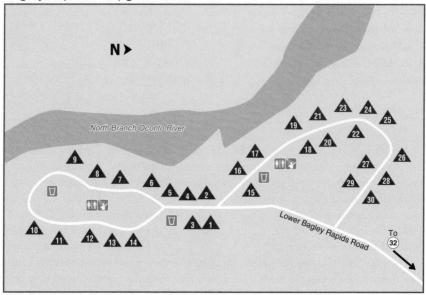

GETTING THERE

From Mountain, drive south on WI 32 for 2 miles to Bagley Rapids Road. Turn right on Bagley Rapids Road and follow it 2 miles to the campground.

GPS COORDINATES: N45° 9.528' W88° 27.947'

38

Bear Lake Campground

Beauty ★★★★ / Privacy ★★★★★ / Spaciousness ★★★ / Quiet ★★★★★ / Security ★★★ / Cleanliness ★★★

Walk-in campsites add even more lakeside overnighting options here.

Isn't life great when we are faced with a win-win choice? Bear Lake Campground provides three distinct camping options: walk-in camping, lakeside camping, or blufftop camping. Each option offers watery vistas and easy access to the campground's namesake, Bear Lake. Of course, after you pick your campsite, you will have to decide whether to fish, swim, canoe, hike, bird-watch, or just relax in the hammock. Oh, life's dilemmas!

First, you must make your campsite decision. Enter Bear Lake Recreation Area and pass the road leading left down to the Bear Lake boat landing. Ahead, the campground road splits. The road to the left leads to campsites 21–27. Campsite 21 is small, open, and probably the least used in the campground, while campsite 22 is large and well shaded and used by larger groups. The other five sites are walk-in sites, accessed by a short trail that passes by the campground swim beach. Parking is available at the small auto turnaround. These walk-in sites are situated on a peninsula that juts into Bear Lake, and all have direct lake access via short foot trails. Campsite 23 is on a cove of the lake and is a bit open. Campsite 24 is more shaded. Campsite 25 overlooks the main body of Bear Lake. Campsite 26 is just a few steps from the water. Campsite 27 stands at the tip of the peninsula and is the most popular site. These campsites have access to a vault toilet also used for the nearby picnic area.

Lakeside camping is one of three options at Bear Lake.   *courtesy of the U.S. Forest Service/public domain*

KEY INFORMATION

CONTACT: USFS Lakewood-Laona Ranger District, 715-674-4481, www.fs.usda.gov /cnnf; reservations 877-444-6777, recreation.gov

OPEN: May–November

SITES: 27

EACH SITE: Picnic table, fire ring

ASSIGNMENT: By phone; internet; or first come, first served

REGISTRATION: Self-registration on-site

FACILITIES: Vault toilets, pump well

PARKING: At campsites only

FEE: $12

ELEVATION: 1,400'

RESTRICTIONS:

PETS: On leash only

FIRES: In fire ring only; firewood must be purchased in state within 10 miles of campground

ALCOHOL: At campsites and at walk-in parking area

VEHICLES: 2/site

OTHER: 14-day stay limit

The remaining sites, nine of which are on bluffs near the lake, lie along a road running parallel to the shoreline of Bear Lake. The mixed forest of hardwoods and many conifers grows dense, especially between campsites, which are average in size and have mostly gravel and dirt for their floors. Campsites 5 and 6 have trails leading to the water. The bluff-top campsites begin past site 9. Campsite 12 is of special note, with steps leading up from the parking spur to a secluded hilltop site. Campsite 13 has maximum solitude away from the lake, and campsite 15 has an awesome blufftop view of the lake. Keep those binoculars handy for loon watching—the birds were visible and calling during my visit. The shoreline curves away, and lake views become scarce past site 17, but campsites 18–20 feature good solitude, both in distance from one another and from the thick vegetation between campsites. A foot trail runs along the shore below the bluff-side campsites. Two water spigots and vault toilets serve the campground.

Adventurous anglers and explorers can check out 5-acre Little Cub Lake, where they can fish for trout. The trail to Little Cub Lake starts on the loop road curving away from the campground. A parking area and trail sign mark the spot. Little Cub Lake is 27 feet at its deepest. If you want to fish nearer to camp, choose 68-acre Bear Lake. It has excellent panfish and northern pike opportunities, and largemouth bass are found in good numbers too. Bear Lake is electric motors only, delivering a peaceful atmosphere. Bear Lake also has one of the best swim beaches in the Chequamegon-Nicolet National Forest. A large, sandy shore is framed by wooden berms, while buoys float in the copper-colored water. Grass flourishes away from the beach.

Two hiking trails require a short drive to reach their trailheads. Continue east beyond the campground on Forest Road 2136 (Goodman Park Road) and travel 1.3 miles to the Halley Creek Bird Trail, created in concert with the Wisconsin Audubon Society. This path makes a mile-long loop that passes through varied bird habitats. To reach the Michigan Rapids Trail, continue east on FR 2136 just a bit beyond the Halley Creek Bird Trail, and then turn left on FR 2134 (Michigan Rapids Road). The trailhead is just south of the bridge on the Peshtigo River. This trail makes a 2-mile loop along the Peshtigo. Check out the rock formations and islands on the river. The Peshtigo is also good for paddling and trout fishing. A 6-mile paddle starts near the Michigan Rapids Trail and heads down to the Burton Wells

Bridge, which can be reached by following FR 2136 east beyond Michigan Rapids Road. You may have to portage Ralton's Rip Rapids, a class III endeavor. The Chequamegon-Nicolet National Forest map comes in handy here—a quick look will show how close all these win-win destinations are.

Bear Lake Campground

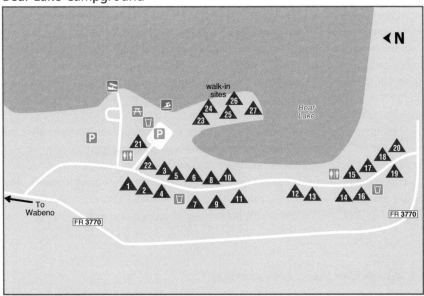

GETTING THERE

From Wabeno, head north on WI 32 for 6 miles to County Road T. Turn right on CR T and go 3 miles to CR H. Turn left on CR H and drive 0.5 mile, and then turn right on FR 2136 (Goodman Park Road). Follow Goodman Park Road 4 miles to FR 3770. Turn right on FR 3770 and reach the campground in 0.3 mile on your left.

GPS COORDINATES: N45° 30.678' W88° 31.824'

39

Goodman Park Campground

Beauty ★★★★ / Privacy ★★★ / Spaciousness ★★★★★ / Quiet ★★★★★ / Security ★★★ / Cleanliness ★★★

Enjoy the view of Strong Falls from a picturesque river bridge.

The Civilian Conservation Corps (CCC) originally developed Goodman Park in the 1930s. Their handiwork added a rustic touch to an already scenic location. Strong Falls loudly crashes among big boulders as the Peshtigo River makes its way downstream to Green Bay. It is along this scenic swath of the Peshtigo that the CCC built beautiful log structures that complement the richly wooded river valley. And the camping here is first rate, especially if you like the sound of rushing water as your evening lullaby. Reservations are available through the Marinette County website listed above.

This county park is one of the best in the state. Covering 240 acres, the locale is culled from the greater Marinette County Forest, which covers more than 220,000 acres. The county forest was established after lands were forfeited in lieu of taxes. Loggers had cutover this part of the state from the 1880s through the 1920s, taking the fantastic stands of white pines so prevalent then. Later, they came back for hardwoods. Farmers eventually moved in from southern Wisconsin, often buying property sight unseen. The soil and terrain were not

A frog's-eye view of the bridge over the Peshtigo River

photographed by Kevin Revolinski

KEY INFORMATION

CONTACT: Marinette County, 715-732-7530, marinettecounty.com/parks

OPEN: May–November; water may be unavailable October–November

SITES: 15

EACH SITE: Picnic table, in-ground fire ring

ASSIGNMENT: First come, first served and by reservation

REGISTRATION: Self-registration on-site

FACILITIES: Vault toilet, pump well

PARKING: At campsites only

FEE: $10

ELEVATION: 1,230'

RESTRICTIONS:

PETS: On leash only

FIRES: In fire ring only

ALCOHOL: No consumption of alcoholic beverages 1–4 a.m.

VEHICLES: 2/site

OTHER: Pack it in; pack it out

conducive to farming, and the land quickly played out. Farmers gave up and left. Marinette County took over the abandoned farmland and began restoring and cultivating the land for what it grew best—trees. Today, the timber industry brings revenue and jobs to Marinette County, which in turn set aside many parks in the special spots of their forest. Marinette County is also the waterfall capital of the state, and while Strong Falls may not be the biggest or the tallest falls, the cascade and surrounding scenery, as well as the quiet, out-of-the-way campground, add up to a great yet often unheralded tent-camping destination.

Pass through the main part of the park and resist the temptation to stop until you have selected your campsite. Enter a loop on high, level ground above the Peshtigo River, which is clearly audible. The pump well is near the fee station. Campsite 1 lies between a widespread oak and a line of red pines. Campsites 2 and 4 are on the inside of the loop in an open, grassy area with a few aspens in the middle. Campsite 3 is large and open too. Here, the loop passes beneath enormous red pines with a mixed understory of spruces and hardwoods, and the campground completely changes character. Campsites 5 and 6 are backed into the tall pines, with red needles covering the ground. Campsite 7 is inside the loop and private. Campsite 8 is L-shaped and private too. A pair of vault toilets is on the inside of the loop.

The loop eventually curves along the river to the best campsites. These are all large sites with red pines growing in and around them, and there is enough greenery between the sites for decent privacy. Trails lead from most campsites down to the river. I stayed in site 12 and had the whole place to myself on a nice July weekday, though there were many day visitors at the falls area.

Once you grab a campsite, head down to Strong Falls. Boulders stand defiant in the copper-colored water. Wide rock slabs border the river. A grassy flat has shade trees and a picnic table along the water. Two rustic lodge buildings and a gazebo border the Peshtigo River. Other charming log structures rest away from the river, including a cabin that can be rented by the night. An arched wooden bridge crosses the Peshtigo and leads to an island where water dances between rocks on the far side. A boardwalk connects to the second bridge to the far bank. Informal paths head along the river and rocks. People like to get sun on the rocks, fish for trout and panfish in pools between the numerous rapids, or simply relax by the gazebo. And relaxing may just be the best thing to do at this fine county park.

Goodman Park Campground

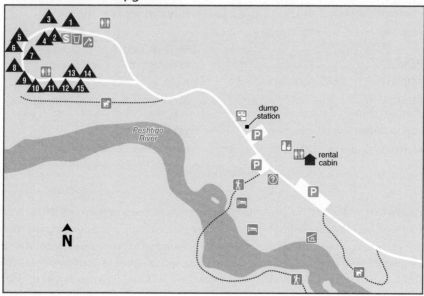

GETTING THERE

From Wabeno, head north on WI 32 for 6 miles to County Road T. Turn right on CR T and follow it 3 miles to CR H. Turn left on CR H and follow it 0.5 mile, and then turn right on Forest Road 2136 (Goodman Park Road). Follow Goodman Park Road 15 miles to Goodman Park Road yet again. (That's not a misprint. The first Goodman Park Road turns into Benson Lake Road upon entering Marinette County.) Turn right on Goodman Park Road for the second time, and follow it 0.5 mile to Goodman Park on your right.

GPS COORDINATES: N45° 31.095' W88° 20.272'

40

⚠ Laura Lake Campground

Beauty ★★★★★ / Privacy ★★★★ / Spaciousness ★★★★★ / Quiet ★★★★★ / Security ★★★★ /
Cleanliness ★★★★

This is a gem of the Chequamegon-Nicolet National Forest.

The Chequamegon-Nicolet National Forest brochure describes Laura Lake this way: "If you could create an ideal campground, what would it include? For setting, maybe it should lie between two beautiful lakes. Of course, the lakes would be clear, with good fishing and excellent swimming. There would need to be a trail circling one of those beautiful lakes for scenic walks. And naturally there would be no development on either lake. Sound perfect? Don't bother creating it. It already exists at Laura Lake."

That's quite a claim, but Laura Lake fully lives up to the U.S. Forest Service's billing. It was a long drive getting there, and I was hoping for the best while pulling in, remembering how other highly touted campgrounds had turned out to be duds. But as I pitched my tent at campsite 10, I was ecstatic at what I saw. I knew that I had found a winner in the great Northwoods of Laura Lake. But campsite 10 is not the only winner here. All the sites are great. The campground is divided into three sections. The first campground road houses sites 1–15, though they appear in reverse order as you enter. Nine of these sites are

Angler on Laura Lake

courtesy of the U.S. Forest Service/public domain

CONTACT: USFS Lakewood-Laona Ranger District, 715-674-4481, www.fs.usda.gov /cnnf, reservations 877-444-6777, recreation.gov

OPEN: Early May–mid-October

SITES: 41

EACH SITE: Picnic table, fire grate

ASSIGNMENT: By phone; internet; or first come, first served

REGISTRATION: Self-registration on-site

FACILITIES: Vault toilets, pump well

PARKING: At campsites only

FEE: $12

ELEVATION: 1,500'

RESTRICTIONS:

PETS: On leash only

FIRES: In fire ring only; firewood must be purchased in state within 10 miles of campground

ALCOHOL: At campsites only

VEHICLES: 2/site

OTHER: 14-day stay limit

stretched along Laura Lake. Overhead is a beautiful mix of maples, paper birches, yellow birches, basswoods, a few oaks, and evergreens—hemlocks, spruces, and balsams. Ferns, grass, and small trees provide ample privacy between the well-separated campsites that are a bit back from the water. However, the water can be easily accessed from your camp. The sites away from the water are even more private and are used less often. A pump well lies at the end of the loop near the small boat launch on Laura Lake.

Campsites 16–26 are stretched along the next campground road. The lakeside sites sit atop a hill. Campers park and take steps down to some of the sites, also located in very attractive woods. Again, the sites away from the water are more private. Campsite 25 is set in the woods away from the water and everyone else. A pump well is located at the beginning of the road. The third area lies at the end of the dead end and houses campsites 27–41. The first few of these are the farthest from the lake but are also widely separated from each other. Campsites 35, 37, and 38 are lakeside.

Vault toilets are conveniently situated throughout the long and narrow campground. Laura Lake often fills on weekends, but this place is special enough to justify a little effort to get here during the week. All campsites can be reserved. A closer look at Laura Lake will reveal the crystal-clear water promised by the U.S. Forest Service. Furthermore, the lake is completely encircled by national forest land, making for an untamed landscape. The 110-acre lake is an "electric motors only" lake, making for a serene experience, sans gas motor noise. Largemouth bass, smallmouth bass, and panfish can be caught from Laura Lake. The 50-acre Gordon Lake, just a walk away, also has a boat ramp. Gordon Lake has largemouth bass, smallmouth bass, and panfish in good numbers. The swim beach here is scenic enough to match the surroundings. A grassy lawn rises from the sand and is complemented by picnic tables. Nearby woods offer shade for those who don't want to be in the water.

The final piece of the puzzle is the Laura Lake Trail. This footpath officially begins near the turn to the Laura Lake boat ramp. It passes the isthmus of land between Gordon Lake and Laura Lake, and then works around to near the shore of Laura Lake, keeping the water in sight. A short spur trail leads north to Bog Lake. A contemplation bench marks the halfway point. Watch for ospreys or loons on the lake. Chances are that you already will have heard a loon by the time you take to the trail.

Laura Lake Campground

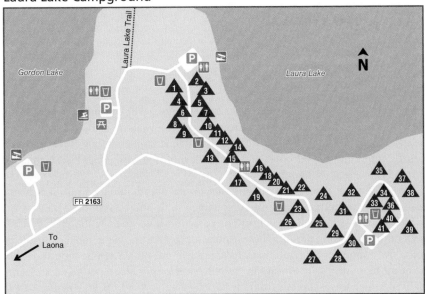

GETTING THERE

From the junction of US 8 and WI 32 in Laona, head north on US 8 for 15.2 miles to Forest Road 2163. Turn left on FR 2163 and follow it 5 miles to a dead end at the campground.

GPS COORDINATES: N45° 42.239' W88° 30.459'

41

⛺ Lauterman Lake and Perch Lake Campgrounds

Beauty ★★★★★ / Privacy ★★★★★ / Spaciousness ★★★★★ / Quiet ★★★★ / Security ★★★ / Cleanliness ★★★★

All the campsites on these two lakes are walk-in!

Campers who place a very high value on campsite privacy will love these two destinations. Lauterman Lake and Perch Lake have been turned into walk-in camping areas that take some effort to get to (anywhere from 200 yards to a mile walk), but they are the most rustic campsites in this entire guidebook, and not to be confused with Perch Lake Campground (see page 116) near Drummond.

Before you come here, check the internet or call ahead and ask to be sent maps for Perch Lake and Lauterman Lake walk-in campgrounds and surrounding trails. You can also inquire about getting an annual parking pass, or just use the pay station at Perch Lake to get your daily parking permit. There is no actual fee for the camping, just for the parking. The five campsites on Lauterman Lake are laid out on a 3.1-mile loop trail, though some of the sites offer shorter ways in. To reach the loop trail, do not take the Beginners Loop Trail, which leaves directly from the parking area. Instead, take the Lauterman Trail, located across the road from the parking area. Continue on the Lauterman Trail until you

Hiking into camp

courtesy of the U.S. Forest Service/public domain

KEY INFORMATION

CONTACT: USFS, 715-528-4464,
tinyurl.com/lauterman

OPEN: Year-round

SITES: Lauterman Lake, 5; Perch Lake, 5

EACH SITE: Picnic table, fire ring;
most sites have vault toilets

ASSIGNMENT: First come, first served

REGISTRATION: No registration

FACILITIES: None

PARKING: At Lauterman Lake and Perch Lake
walk-in parking areas

FEE: $5 daily parking fee

ELEVATION: 1,450'

RESTRICTIONS:

PETS: On leash only

FIRES: In fire ring only; firewood must be
purchased in state within 10 miles of
campground

ALCOHOL: At campsites only

VEHICLES: No restrictions

OTHER: 14-day stay limit

reach a junction. For sites 1–3, follow the trail indicating the best direction, which leads right. (Walk left to reach sites 4 and 5.) Circle around and come to the trail leading left to site 1, which is perched on a grassy hill with limited shade. A side trail leads a short distance to WI 70. You could walk to the site from the parking area, find the campsite, and then drop your gear near WI 70 via car (making for a shorter carry), but the proximity of WI 70 is the downside of this site. The trail continues and splits. The uphill route leads to site 2 on a shaded knob with a trail leading down to the water. You can reach site 3 by continuing down the trail, but most people use Forest Road 2553, one road west of the Lauterman parking area. From here, a 200-yard trail leads up to a beautiful, level site under hardwoods and above the lake. This is the most popular campsite on Lauterman Lake.

To reach sites 4 and 5, turn left at the junction mentioned above. Campsite 4 is on the south end of the lake near a shelter built for cross-country skiers. The shelter could come in handy during a rain. Campsite 5 is the least used, as the lake is a little more difficult to reach from there.

The five campsites on Perch Lake are laid out on a 1.3-mile loop trail that encircles the lake. Leave the Perch Lake parking area and climb over a hill. Turn right on the loop (left for unit 5) and soon come to site 1. It is well shaded and near the canoe/kayak launch, making for quick and easy water access. Campers heading to other sites could paddle their gear across the lake to ease gear toting. Site 2 is on a point. Site 3 is perched on a hill and is the least popular, being too open and far above the lake. Site 4 is close to the water and is shaded by big maples. Don't be surprised if you hear loons; they nest on Perch Lake. Site 5 is close to the lake in a mix of sun and shade. It has easy water access to a gravel shore and is ideal for canoes and kayaks. Fishing paddlers and shore anglers can vie for northern pike, bass, and bluegill on this 51-acre lake. At 44 acres, Lauterman Lake offers fishing for muskie, bass, and panfish.

Lauterman Lake Campground never fills, and Perch Lake Campground very rarely fills. Come here anytime for a great getaway. If you are here visiting Whisker Lake Wilderness, try to come in spring or fall—the trails will be less overgrown. The Lauterman trail system, which includes the Perch Lake Loop Trail and many others, is mown and/or otherwise well maintained. The Lauterman Lake National Recreation Trail is 9 miles long; it and many other connecting paths are depicted on the U.S. Forest Service's Lauterman Lake National Recreation Trail map. Mountain bikers and hikers will enjoy the undulating, mostly forested path with boardwalks over wetlands. A trail connects Lauterman Lake to Perch Lake. The 2.8-mile Porky Trail loops from the shelter near Lauterman site 4. The Chipmunk Trail leads beyond the Porky Trail all the way to the Pine River. The trailhead for Whisker Lake Wilderness is 0.6 mile north of the Perch Lake parking area. Here, you can head for Riley Lake and Riley Creek for some backwoods trout fishing.

Lauterman Lake and Perch Lake Campgrounds

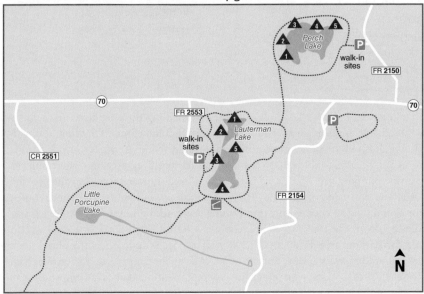

GETTING THERE

From Cavour, head north on WI 139 for 21 miles to WI 70. Turn right (east) on WI 70 and follow it 8.2 miles to Forest Road 2154. Turn right on FR 2154, and the Lauterman Lake parking area is on your left. To reach Perch Lake, keep forward on WI 70 for 0.3 mile beyond FR 2154, and turn left on FR 2150. Follow FR 2150 for 0.5 mile to reach the Perch Lake parking area, on your left.

GPS COORDINATES:
LAUTERMAN LAKE N45° 55.045' W88° 30.929'
PERCH LAKE N45° 55.456' W88° 29.809'

42

⚠ Lost Lake Campground

Beauty ★★★★ / Privacy ★★★ / Spaciousness ★★★★ / Quiet ★★★★ / Security ★★★ / Cleanliness ★★★

Old-growth trees border this spring-fed lake.

Lost Lake got its name for having no visible inflow or outlet to the body of water. The water in this lake has nowhere to go, and thus the water has lost its way. Tall white pines and other evergreens border the deep, cool lake, which is fed by underground springs, making a good place even better. Many of these trees are old growth. A hiking trail runs in their shadows. At Lost Lake, you can camp in a fine shoreline setting and enjoy these natural assets and others concentrated in the area.

The campsites are strung along a road running atop a low rise by the lake. Most campsites are well shaded. The sites abutting the lake dip toward the water. Not all are perfectly level. Sixteen of the 27 campsites face Lost Lake. Campsite 1 is narrow, open, and grassy, and it is usually the last to be taken. A forest of maples, aspens, birches, and a few evergreens begins just past this site. Campsite 7 is large and inside the loop. Beyond here, many campsites bordering the lake are two-tiered—the parking area is on one level and the tent site, picnic table, and fire ring are just a short walk below. These two-tiered sites are mostly large and close to the lake with short paths meeting a hiking trail that runs parallel to the shoreline between the water and the campsites. The hardwood leaves overhead are so dense in places that only grass, ferns, and small trees grow beneath them. This attractive look does compromise campsite privacy, however. The campsites become more widely spaced

Paddling fun on Lost Lake

KEY INFORMATION

CONTACT: USFS Eagle River–Florence Ranger District, 715-528-4464, www.fs.usda.gov/cnnf

OPEN: Early May–mid-October

SITES: 28

EACH SITE: Picnic table, fire ring

ASSIGNMENT: First come, first served

REGISTRATION: Self-registration on-site

FACILITIES: Vault toilets, water spigot, pump well

PARKING: At campsites only

FEE: $12

ELEVATION: 1,525'

RESTRICTIONS:

PETS: On leash only

FIRES: In fire ring only; firewood must be purchased in state within 10 miles of campground

ALCOHOL: At campsites only

VEHICLES: 2/site

OTHER: 21-day stay limit

---

after campsite 16. After the access road turns away from Lost Lake, the campsites get even larger. Basswoods and maples shade the last five campsites nearly every minute of the day. Lost Lake generally fills only on holiday weekends, but the lakeside sites are scooped up by mid-Saturday on every weekend. Vault toilets and water sources are immediately available in the campground.

A fine picnic area lies next to the boat landing under some hemlocks. No gas or electric motors are allowed on this serene lake. Anglers can vie for trout, bass, and panfish. A sandy swim beach is located on the shore of Lost Lake about midway along the campground. Buoys delineate the swim area. The Pine River lies just north of Lost Lake and offers stream fishing for native brook trout. Access is at Chipmunk Rapids Campground—a fine place to tent, but it has only six sites. Chipmunk Rapids also has an artesian well with the finest drinking water in northeast Wisconsin. You ought to check it out. The Pine River, a Wisconsin Wild River, can also be paddled. A good 6-mile canoe or kayak run can be made from the bridge at WI 139 down to Chipmunk Rapids Campground. The river gets tougher downstream of Chipmunk Rapids, and portages are required. Check water flow before undertaking this paddle in later summer.

The hiking around Lost Lake is some of the best in the Chequamegon-Nicolet National Forest. The Assessor's Interpretive Trail leaves from near the end of the campground and makes a 1-mile loop beneath those impressive old-growth white pines and hemlocks. Of special note is the Assessor White Pine, a tree preserved at the behest of a taxman. Learn the full story on this not-to-be-missed interpretive path. I was very impressed with the Ridge Trail, which makes a 3.8-mile loop from the campground. First, it heads over to Chipmunk Rapids, and then it takes you along the Pine River, where you can gain glimpses of the rocky stream. The trail then turns away from the river on a narrow, spindly ridgeline that drops off nearly vertically for quite a distance. The path then descends from the ridge and returns to Lost Lake amid more of those beautiful hemlocks. White rectangles mark the trail, making sure that you won't get lost at Lost Lake.

Lost Lake Campground

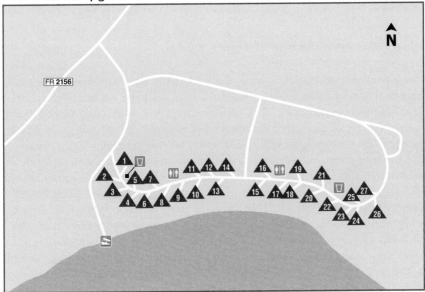

GETTING THERE

From Cavour, head north on WI 139 for 21 miles to WI 70. Turn right (east) on WI 70 and follow it 3.6 miles to Forest Road 2450 (Dream Lake Road). Follow FR 2450, and keep straight (the name changes to Chipmunk Rapids Road and then Lost Lake Road/FR 2156) 6 miles to the campground, on your left.

GPS COORDINATES: N45° 53.008' W88° 33.529'

43

⚠ Luna–White Deer Lake Campground

Beauty ★★★★★ / Privacy ★★★★ / Spaciousness ★★★★ / Quiet ★★★★★ / Security ★★★ / Cleanliness ★★★★

Two scenic lakes are available here for your enjoyment.

Mother Nature was working overtime in this neck of the Wisconsin woods. The two lakes adjacent to this campground, White Deer Lake and Luna Lake, are among the prettiest in the state, and that is saying a lot. They both have ultraclear water, undeveloped shorelines of varied forest types, and some hilly terrain that adds vertical variation to the landscape. Speaking of hills, the campground here is set atop a hill that has campsites overlooking both lakes. From your perch, you will want to see more of the water below. And exploring White Deer Lake and Luna Lake is easy, with boat launches and hiking trails—some of the finest around—circling both of them.

Pass the road leading left and downhill to the swim beach on White Deer Lake before entering the campground. A road to the left leads to a circular loop holding campsites 1–9. A rich forest of cherry, spruce, fir, and maple trees thrives on a hill. Campsite 2 is a bi-level site, with steps leading to a tent pad. Descend a bit and reach sites overlooking White Deer Lake. The sites with red-banded posts (sites 5 and 7) have the lake view and the higher price. Steep trails lead down to the water. Campsites 6 and 9 are inside the loop but are heavily shaded. Spindly understory trees grow so tightly that it's hard to walk among them, making for good campsite privacy.

Motors are not allowed on Luna and White Deer Lakes.

courtesy of the U.S. Forest Service/public domain

KEY INFORMATION

CONTACT: USFS Eagle River–Florence Ranger District, 715-479-2827, www.fs.usda.gov/cnnf

OPEN: May–third weekend in October

SITES: 37

EACH SITE: Picnic table, fire grate

ASSIGNMENT: First come, first served

REGISTRATION: Self-registration on-site

FACILITIES: Vault toilets, pump wells

PARKING: At campsites only

FEE: $12 ($15 lake-view site)

ELEVATION: 1,700'

RESTRICTIONS:

PETS: On leash only

FIRES: In fire ring only; firewood must be purchased in state within 10 miles of campground

ALCOHOL: At campsites only

VEHICLES: 3/site

OTHER: 14-day stay limit

The second loop is long and narrow, stretched along the strip of land between the two lakes. Campsites 12 and 14 are very close to Luna Lake but have limited views because of the dense forest. A huge yellow birch grows behind campsite 14. Stately hemlocks circled my campsite at 16; these trees are prevalent throughout the area. Campsites 17 and 19 are hilltop sites looking out on Luna Lake. The loop curves around to the left, and the sites on the outside of the loop now overlook White Deer Lake. Some of these sites are a bit sloped but are still among the first to be scooped up. Two large, level sites, 25 and 26, are inside the loop. Rocks and red pines become more prevalent near campsite 27, which is a pull-beside site. Campsites 28 and 29 are on their own road, bisecting the oblong loop. Most of the last eight campsites are lake-view sites. They are fairly large and well separated, offering great privacy aided by the hilly nature of the campground. Campsite 37 is shaded by a large maple in the middle. Surprisingly, this gem of a campground fills only erratically, but sites are usually open on nonholiday weekends. Get here fairly early on Friday, and you should get a site with no problem.

The no-motor lakes offer such attractive paddling and exploring opportunities that you may not even care if the fish aren't biting. Both lakes have largemouth and smallmouth bass as well as panfish. White Deer Lake is purported to have trout, too, and at 62 acres and a maximum depth of 45 feet, they could indeed be in there somewhere. Luna Lake is 67 acres in size. You may want to get the lay of the land and lakes before you toss in a line. The Luna–White Deer Trail makes a 4-mile figure-eight loop around both lakes, and it can be shortened to a pair of 2-mile hikes for quicker getaways. Both loops traverse by sun-splashed sandy shores, beneath tall red pines on steep hillsides, through hardwood forests with grass and ferns galore, under dark hemlock thickets, and across wetlands via wooden bridges. The portion along Luna Lake also passes two rustic campsites across from the campground. Part of the Hidden Lakes Trail system, the Luna–White Deer Trail connects ambitious hikers with the 13-mile Hidden Lakes Trail Loop that heads over to Franklin Lake Campground and into remote backcountry areas. Major trail intersections are signed. Make time on your camping adventure to at least hike around Luna Lake or White Deer Lake if you aren't up to the Hidden Lakes Trail Loop.

The swim beach has a good natural setting. A little trail leads to this grassy locale shaded by pines. Wooden berms circle a developed sand beach, and secured buoys delineate a swimming area that's about as clear as you'll find in the state. After a visit here, you also will be clear about how hard Mother Nature worked on this slice of the Chequamegon-Nicolet National Forest.

Luna-White Deer Lake Campground

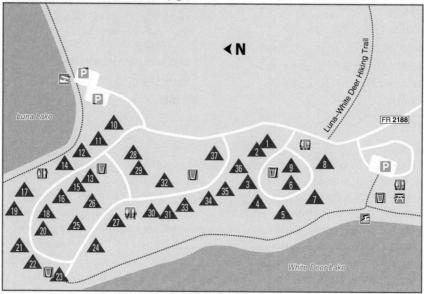

GETTING THERE

From the intersection of US 45 and WI 70 on the east end of Eagle River, near the Eagle River Ranger Station, take WI 70 east 14 miles to Forest Road 2176. Turn right on FR 2176 and follow it 6 miles to FR 2168. Turn right on FR 2188 and follow it 0.8 mile to the campground.

GPS COORDINATES: N45° 53.994' W88° 57.725'

44

Newport State Park Campground

Beauty ★★★★ / Privacy ★★★★★ / Spaciousness ★★★★ / Quiet ★★★★★ / Security ★★★★ /
Cleanliness ★★★★

It is a delight to hit some of the little touristy towns along WI 42 and then disappear into wilderness where you may not see another soul.

Sister state parks here in Door County—Potawatomi and Peninsula—are certainly quite popular for tent camping and are excellent bets in this popular peninsular destination. However, what these parks can't offer by comparison to Newport are peace and solitude. The trade-off is the additional effort required: carrying all your gear from the parking areas to one of the 17 secluded—and reservable—hike-in sites along the shores of Lake Michigan. Well worth it, I'd say.

This stunning slice of unadulterated terrain seems much farther from the madding crowd than it is because of its 11 miles of shoreline, with wilderness coming right up to the beaches of sand, gravel, stone, or cobble. You'd never guess that this land was once clear-cut for farming and then again for commercial lumber in the early 20th century. It is a delight to hit some of the little touristy towns along WI 42 and then disappear into wilderness, where you may not see another soul.

Fall foliage makes hiking a treat at Newport State Park.
photographed by RJ and Linda Miller/courtesy of TravelWisconsin.com

KEY INFORMATION

CONTACT: Wisconsin Department of Natural Resources, 920-854-2500, dnr.wi.gov /topic/parks/name/newport; reservations 888-WI-PARKS, wisconsin.goingtocamp.com

OPEN: Year-round

SITES: 17

EACH SITE: Pit toilet (no toilet paper!), fire ring and grill, metal food storage box, benches

ASSIGNMENT: By phone; internet; or first come, first served

REGISTRATION: At park office or self-register

FACILITIES: Pit toilets, water at parking lot

PARKING: At parking area or along Europe Bay Road

FEE: Wisconsin residents, $20; nonresidents, $25; plus vehicle admission fee (Wisconsin residents, $8; nonresidents, $11; Wisconsin residents age 65 and older, $3); $7.75 reservation fee

ELEVATION: 623'

RESTRICTIONS:

PETS: On leash only

FIRES: In fire ring or grill only; firewood must be purchased in state within 10 miles of campground

ALCOHOL: Allowed

VEHICLES: No restrictions; except on Europe Bay Road, 1/site

OTHER: 14-day stay limit

When checking in at the contact station, visit the interpretive center inside, which features a menagerie of mounted native wildlife and information on geological history, including samples of coral formed more than 425 million years ago.

Three parking lots serve the park, and the distances to each of the sites vary. Sites 14–16 are a 3-mile hike from lot 3, but parking is allowed on Europe Bay Road—a public road that enters the north end of the park—cutting the trek by more than half.

With the exception of sites 1, 2, and 13, which rest on the inside of their respective trails, as well as site 6, campsites sit close to the lake's edge, presenting aquatic vistas. Site 6 is a wooded site and has no lake access. Sites 3, 6, and 15 are the only sites that cannot be reserved.

One of the most popular sites is site 16 at the north end of the park; it rests on a sand dune overlooking Lake Michigan. Site 14 is also north but on the shores of Europe Lake, a warm, shallow, sandy-bottomed lake less than a quarter-mile inland from chilly watered Lake Michigan. Site 15 also borders the smaller body of water.

Privacy is premium at this campground, and there are no sites that look out upon another. Thimbleberry bushes provide even more cover and also some delectable treats in early August. (Site 12 has the biggest abundance of the raspberry-like berries.) All are nicely shaded. Sites 10 and 12 offer a bit more sun, and 10 faces south over a gravel shoreline. Sites 3 and 4 overlook Duck Bay, which can be odoriferous in spring when an abundance of algae moves in to shore.

Each pair of sites shares a pit toilet, but don't forget to bring your own toilet paper. Porcupines and raccoons can sometimes be a nuisance, but the steel storage boxes provided at each site should take care of that.

The sites fill up on weekends mid-May–October; even during the week in July and August, it may be hard to get a spot without a reservation. During these times, you may be at one site one night and have to switch to another the next if you haven't reserved. Camping is allowed year-round except during deer hunting season. The season generally occurs nine days around Thanksgiving, when you are not going to want to wander around the woods without blaze-orange clothing on.

Each site is limited to six campers or one family. Larger groups can use the group camp, which rests in open woods only 0.4 mile from parking lot 3. The beach at parking lot 3 offers a picnic area with grills, tables, restrooms, and changing stalls but no lifeguard.

Fifteen of the 28 miles of trails are open to mountain bikers. The most challenging and most popular is Rowleys Trail, which passes just along the shore facing west into Rowleys Bay.

Newport is the best place to experience solitude in Door County without leaving the mainland. But its proximity to the main highway means that you can still visit the tourist attractions without too much effort if you'd like.

Newport State Park Campground

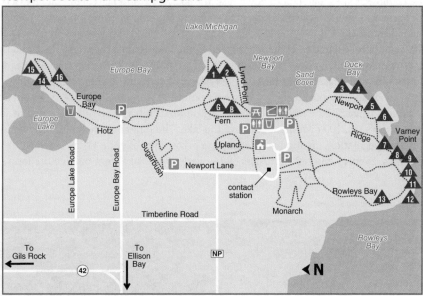

GETTING THERE

From WI 42, 3 miles east of Ellison Bay, turn south on County Road NP and follow it to its end where it intersects Newport Lane. Take this to the right to the park entrance.

GPS COORDINATES: N45° 14.071' W86° 59.892'

45

North Trout Lake Campground

Beauty ★★★★ / Privacy ★★★ / Spaciousness ★★★★ / Quiet ★★★ / Security ★★★★ / Cleanliness ★★★

Shady camping atop a piney bluff awaits visitors to this big lake.

Trout Lake is big—3,816 acres to be exact. And out of all that shoreline, Northern Highland–American Legion State Forest personnel may have picked the prettiest spot of all to develop North Trout Lake Campground. Here, the shoreline rises high up a hill covered in mixed pines. Campsites are situated both down near the lake and atop a high bluff that gives a commanding view of this fish-filled lake. So grab your tent (and maybe some binoculars) and head on up to Trout Lake.

The campground makes a big loop divided in the middle. Pass the wood shed, and three walk-in tent campsites are in a pine-dotted flat to your left. These large campsites offer good lake views and access but have limited privacy due to minimal understory. Enter the campground loop. Campsites 1–4 are also in a piney flat with excellent lake views but again have limited privacy. Pine needles carpet the ground. Climb a steep hill and come to some neat blufftop sites, 100 or more feet above the lake. The pines are thick here, and so is the understory vegetation, creating good campsite privacy yet offering vistas between the tall tree trunks. Even-numbered campsites 6–14 overlook the lake from outside the loop. The

Relax on Trout Lake's shoreline.

photographed by Robert Kramer

KEY INFORMATION

CONTACT: Wisconsin Department of Natural Resources, 715-385-2727, dnr.wi.gov/topic/stateforests/nhal

OPEN: Opens and closes with snow conditions; pump well open Memorial Day weekend–Labor Day weekend

SITES: 48

EACH SITE: Picnic table, fire ring

ASSIGNMENT: First come, first served

REGISTRATION: Attendant will come by and register you

FACILITIES: Vault toilets, pump wells

PARKING: At campsites only

FEE: Wisconsin residents, $16; nonresidents, $21; plus vehicle admission fee (Wisconsin residents, $8; nonresidents, $11; Wisconsin residents age 65 and older, $3)

ELEVATION: 1,625'

RESTRICTIONS:

PETS: On leash only

FIRES: In fire ring only; firewood must be purchased in state within 10 miles of campground

ALCOHOL: At campsites only

VEHICLES: No restrictions

OTHER: 21-day stay limit

---

odd-numbered inside-loop campsites are shaded and fine, but they don't offer the blufftop vistas that the even-numbered sites do. Reach the parking area for North Trout Lake's walk-in tent campsites. A foot trail leads steeply off the bluff down to a second flat, where walk-in sites 15–19 lie beside Trout Lake. Pines shade these sites. The sites are a bit close together for walk-in sites, but I would be proud to pitch my tent at any one of them. Campsite 19 is the most secluded and is set away from the lake. Campsite 20 is a drive-up site all by itself. The road cutting through the loop houses very shady sites, 21–31, that work especially well for privacy seekers. The sites are quite widespread for being in the middle of a loop (save for campsites 30 and 31, which are too close together). The outside of the loop holds campsites 32–45. Pass the North Trout Nature Trail and reach campsite 32. Evergreens add a scenic touch to the shady campsites here. Two pairs of campsites are double sites for larger groups. The last four sites are off the bluff in a piney flat. The sites are nice but lack privacy and are a little close to the action. They do offer quick access to the water.

It is not all about water here at Trout Lake, though. The North Trout Nature Trail leaves directly from the campground. The path makes a 1-mile loop around a mature black spruce–tamarack bog and along North Trout Lake. But that is not the only trail around here. A paved bike trail leads north, roughly paralleling County Road M, to the town of Boulder Junction. That way you can leave your car at the campground for those supply runs. The paved bike trail also leads south to Crystal Lake Campground and Saynor, over by Plum Lake. If you make it to Saynor, you will be plum tired.

Trout Lake obviously harbors its namesake, as it is 117 feet at its deepest. Besides trout, Trout Lake offers anglers muskellunge, northern pike, walleye, bass, and panfish. A boat landing, as well as a water-access area, is conveniently close to the campground. This spot near the boat landing has a nice swim beach. A grassy area, partly shaded, offers a place to relax and take in the scenery and action. Boats are often tooling around Trout Lake for recreation and to fish. And they have plenty of water to cover, considering the acreage of Trout Lake.

North Trout Lake Campground

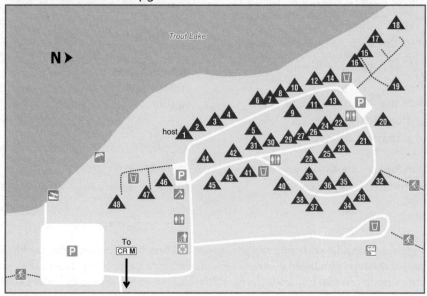

GETTING THERE

From the intersection of US 51 and WI 47 in Woodruff, take US 51 north 6.2 miles to County Road M. Turn right on CR M and travel 6.8 miles to the campground, on your left.

GPS COORDINATES: N46° 03.867' W89° 38.756'

46

Rock Island State Park Campground

Beauty ★★★★★ / Privacy ★★★★★ / Spaciousness ★★★★ / Quiet ★★★★★ / Security ★★★★★ /
Cleanliness ★★★★

It takes a lot of effort to reach Rock Island, but your determination will be worth it.

Some claim that the best of the best tent camping is on Rock Island, famed as Wisconsin's northeasternmost point. A tent-camping trip to this island park, located two ferry rides northeast of the tip of the Door Peninsula, may leave you nodding your head in agreement. Once the home of wealthy inventor Chester H. Thordarson, Rock Island comprises 900 acres of history and nature, where beaches, bluffs, and woodlands contrast with the relics of voyageurs, settlers, and parts of Thordarson's estate. The campground here lives up to its heady surroundings.

Campers visiting here live on ferry time. Most who visit are at the mercy of the ferryboat schedule. Be sure to bring all your gear and food (there are no stores on the island) and come ready to walk because no cars are allowed. You will have to tote your gear anywhere from 200 yards to 0.5 mile. I recommend staying at least two nights, given all the effort it takes to reach Rock Island.

This sand beach on Lake Michigan beckons you to Rock Island State Park.

photographed by Princely Nesadurai/courtesy of TravelWisconsin.com

KEY INFORMATION

CONTACT: 920-847-2235, dnr.wi.gov/topic /parks/name/rockisland; reservations 888-WI-PARKS, wisconsin.goingtocamp.com

OPEN: Year-round; private ferry services run only Memorial Day–Columbus Day

SITES: 35

EACH SITE: Picnic table, fire ring

ASSIGNMENT: By phone; internet; or first come, first served

REGISTRATION: At visitor center

FACILITIES: Pit toilets, water spigots

PARKING: At the Jackson Hooper parking lot on Washington Island

FEE: Wisconsin residents, $20; nonresidents, $25; $7.75 reservation fee; round-trip ferries to both Washington and Rock Islands, $25 adults, children $12.50; plus $27 vehicle fee

ELEVATION: 600'

RESTRICTIONS:

PETS: On leash only

FIRES: In fire ring only; firewood must be purchased in state within 10 miles of campground

ALCOHOL: At campsites only

VEHICLES: No vehicles or bicycles in park

OTHER: 21-day stay limit; 6 people/site

Debark the second ferry, walk past buildings from the Thordarson Estate, and pass the water spigot for the campground. Walk between impressive rock walls. Ahead, three trails lead to various parts of the campground. Michigan Avenue leads toward sites 1–12. Pass pit toilets and a changing station at the end of Michigan Avenue. A big dune separates you from Lake Michigan on the southwest shore of Rock Island. Campsites 1–3 are in cedar, sugar maple, and oak woods just inland from a sandy shoreline. Campsites 4–7 are a bit back from the water near an old cemetery. All these sites are near an old Potawatomi village and a building site of the voyageur LaSalle. Campsites 9, 11, and 13 are just on the back side of the dune in a mix of sun and shade.

A grassy trail leads into thick cedar woods atop a bluff. Campsites 15–19 are on the edge of the bluff, providing a stunning vista of Lake Michigan. Campsites 20 and 22 are a bit back from the water, while site 21 offers lake views. Next comes a line of campsites, 23–29, directly beside the water toward Washington Island. This line offers great sites in a mix of sun and shade on the edge of a rock beach.

The third trail leads inland toward heavily wooded, well-separated sites, 30–35, offering maximum solitude. These sites are large and fine, and while they are the last ones taken, they provide shelter when the weather is cool and windy. By the way, a stone shelter building with a fireplace inside lies near the campground for bad-weather days. Six vault toilets are spread throughout the campground. All campsites can be reserved Memorial Day–Columbus Day. Rock Island will fill on Memorial Day weekend, on the last two weekends of July, and most days in August. Chilly winds blowing off Lake Michigan keep campers away early in the season. Consider coming in September.

Some campers shore-fish for smallmouth bass and perch, but the sand and rock beaches are the big draw at Rock Island State Park. No wonder—they offer picture-postcard scenery. The trail system explores some of the human and natural history of the island. Everyone likes to take the mile walk to the Potawatomi Lighthouse. Built in 1836, it is the oldest lighthouse in Wisconsin. The 6.2-mile Thordarson Loop Trail continues beyond the lighthouse around the perimeter of the island to the old fishing village (the first settlement in Door

County), where a water tower and settler house foundations can still be seen. The Algonquin Nature Trail Loop details the flora and lake history of the island. Check out the rock carvings on the bluffs just below the campground. The Viking Hall stands over a beautiful stone boathouse, part of the Thordarson Estate. In here, you can check out artifacts from the days of the Potawatomi tribe to a more recent past, including old photos and some of Thordarson's original Icelandic carved-oak furniture.

Rock Island State Park Campground

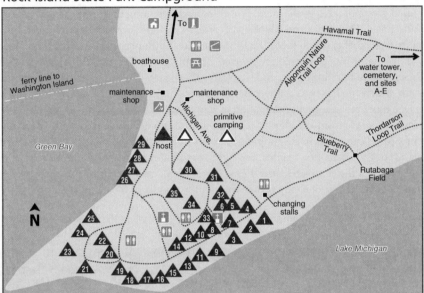

GETTING THERE

From Sturgeon Bay, head north on WI 42 for 46 miles to its end. Here, take a pay ferry (wisferry.com) to reach Washington Island.

From there, drive north on Lobdells Point Road 1.7 miles to Main Road. Turn left on Main Road and follow it 2.6 miles to Jackson Harbor Road. Turn right and follow it 3.6 miles to the Rock Island Ferry. Campers must park in the state lot, just north of the passenger-only pay ferry.

GPS COORDINATES: N45° 24.009' W86° 51.264'

47

⚠ Sandy Beach Lake Campground

Beauty ★★★★ / Privacy ★★★★ / Spaciousness ★★★ / Quiet ★★★★ / Security ★★★★ / Cleanliness ★★★★

The campground at this good swimming lake rarely fills.

Northern Highland–American Legion State Forest was established in 1925 to protect the headwaters of many Wisconsin rivers. This area has the most abundant and closely concentrated group of lakes in the state. From this agglomeration of more than 900 lakes flow the Wisconsin, Flambeau, and Manitowish riverways. One such protected headwater lake is Sandy Beach Lake, which feeds the Flambeau River. After seeing Sandy Beach Lake, you may think that it was protected for its scenic beauty alone. Spruces, firs, pines, and white birches ring the shoreline of this undeveloped lake, and its dark waters contrast with the tan sand for which the lake was named. Being distant from the North Country tourist towns keeps it a quiet tent-camping destination in this vast, 222,000-acre state forest.

The campground sits on a level parcel of thick forestland adjacent to Sandy Beach Lake. The first set of campsites in the loop, 1–13, is situated away from the lake. A dense forest of paper birches, spruces, firs, maples, and hemlocks shades from above. The woods are even thicker between the campsites than they are over them, making for great campsite privacy. Campsite 11 has a pair of shady spruce trees in the middle of the campsite. Campsite 12 is

Check out the Little Bohemia Lodge in nearby Manitowish Waters, where the FBI had a shootout with the John Dillinger Gang in 1934.

photographed by Rick Donaldson

KEY INFORMATION

CONTACT: Wisconsin Department of Natural Resources, 715-385-2727, dnr.wi.gov /topic/StateForests/nhal; reservations 888-WI-PARKS, wisconsin.goingtocamp.com

OPEN: Wednesday before Memorial Day– Tuesday after Columbus Day weekend

SITES: 33

EACH SITE: Picnic table, fire ring

ASSIGNMENT: By phone; internet; or first come, first served

REGISTRATION: Campground host will register you

FACILITIES: Vault toilets, pump wells

PARKING: At campsites only

FEE: Wisconsin residents, $16; nonresidents, $21; plus vehicle admission fee (Wisconsin residents, $8; nonresidents, $11; Wisconsin residents age 65 and older, $3); $7.75 reservation fee

ELEVATION: 1,600'

RESTRICTIONS:

PETS: On leash only

FIRES: In fire ring only; firewood must be purchased in state within 10 miles of campground

ALCOHOL: At campsites only

VEHICLES: No restrictions

OTHER: 21-day stay limit

---

the only sunny site here. The loop curves around and reaches the three walk-in tent campsites, 14–16. Sites 15 and 16 are directly lakeside. Just past the walk-in sites are the coveted lakeside sites. The lakeside sites are large, accommodating a tent, bug-screen shelter, and a small boat, and many red pines provide shade. There are seven drive-up lakeside sites. Two other sites are close to the lake, but lush woods obscure the water view. The sites on the inside of the loop are smaller but will do, though I would just as soon camp in the more private sites, 1–11, at the beginning of the loop if a lakeside site was not available.

A campground host lives on-site for your convenience and safety. Two water spigots and three vault toilets serve the campground. Sandy Beach Lake fills only on holiday weekends and sometimes not even then. However, some campsites can be reserved. Be advised that the mosquitoes can be troublesome early in the camping season.

The lakeside sites are perfect for beach lovers, who can enjoy the sandy waters directly from their campsite. Campers without lakefront sites can walk a short distance to the water access and picnic area, where a grassy flat pocked with pines overlooks a developed swim beach with deep-water buoys. Though the dark-water lake is only 111 acres, gas motors are allowed. Anglers can vie for muskellunge, pike, walleye, largemouth bass, and panfish. Many campers leave their boats directly in front of the campsite. Others use the boat launch located near the campground entrance. The launch also has a small dock. A trail located in pines near the swim beach parking area will lead anglers to Mud Lake, where you can fish for bass in a wild setting. Another fishing option is on the Manitowish River, located just north of Sandy Beach Lake near US 51. It also offers good paddling and fishing opportunities.

Wildlife watching is easy here with Powell Marsh State Wildlife Area just a few miles away. Turn left out of Sandy Beach Road, and follow Powell Marsh Road a few miles to a cleared overlook on your right. The wildlife area offers great views of this home for sandhill cranes and other birdlife. Explorers will want to hike the dikes in this open, watery country. Hikers can also trek the cross-country ski trails located just a short distance from Sandy Beach Road on Powell Marsh Road. Bicyclers can tool around the paved campground road and the road to the swim beach or follow the old Chicago and Northwestern railroad grade near the campground. (You passed over it on the way in, near the junction of Sandy Beach Road and Powell Marsh Road.) Pedal north to Mercer or south to the Lac du Flambeau Reservation. This trail is popular with snowmobiles in the winter. With the attractiveness of Sandy Beach Lake, I think that the campground should be more popular with campers in summer.

Sandy Beach Lake Campground

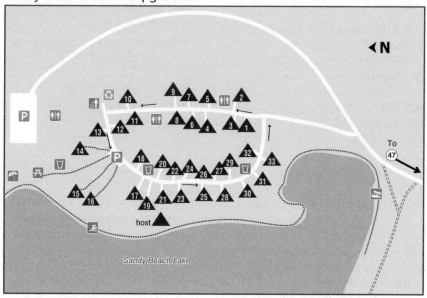

GETTING THERE

From the intersection of US 51 and WI 47 in Woodruff, head north on WI 47 for 23.6 miles, passing through Lac du Flambeau on the way to Powell Marsh Road. Turn right on Powell Marsh Road and follow it 0.2 mile to Sandy Beach Road. Turn left on Sandy Beach Road and follow it 1 mile to reach the campground on your right.

GPS COORDINATES: N46° 6.247' W89° 58.022'

48

⛺ Starrett Lake Campground

Beauty ★★★★ / Privacy ★★★★ / Spaciousness ★★★ / Quiet ★★★★★ / Security ★★★ / Cleanliness ★★★★

Camp beneath the pines on quiet Starrett Lake.

No gas motors are allowed at Starrett Lake—at least not on your boat. This rule sets the tone for this campground: peace and quiet come first. The land encircling Starrett Lake is owned by the Northern Highland–American Legion State Forest, further making the lake a natural respite. Busy roads are far from earshot. The campground, mostly set in a towering pine forest with secluded campsites, adds to the overall serenity of this Northwoods getaway.

The campground lies along the shores of Starrett Lake. Enter the camping area from North Muskellunge Road, and dead ahead you'll see the boat landing, a pump well, and the beach-access area. Head left and come to two small loops. Red pines and jack pines grow high overhead, and maples, oaks, and young trees reach partway up the pines, screening most campers from one another. Pass by campsites 1, 2, and 4, situated beside the lake-access area, and then reach campsites 5 and 6. All five sites are coveted lakefront campsites. Reach the walk-in tent-site parking area, where a short path leads downhill to walk-in sites 9–11, also on the lake. Campsite 10 is beneath a huge white pine. Campsite 11 is a little too open to the sun. Return to the main drive-up campsites and continue to site 12, resting all by itself. Take the other loop in this section of the campground, and curve around to reach widely separated sites with piney floors away from the lake. The brush is thick between sites. I enjoyed campsite 19. Campsite 23 is banked against a hill and offers a nice dose of solitude.

To reach the other half of the campground, head right from the main entrance and reach three walk-in tent sites. While these sites are usually the first to go, they may be a little too close to the lake action for some, as the boat ramp and water-access areas are nearby. All three sites are large and shady, however. Keep driving to the loop to find other sites that are more typical of what campers expect of walk-in sites. Enter the final loop. More hardwoods grow in this hilly area. Campsites 34–37 are

Serene Starrett Lake
photographed by Jen AnneTastic

KEY INFORMATION

CONTACT: Wisconsin Department of Natural Resources, 715-385-2727, dnr.wi.gov/topic/StateForests/nhal

OPEN: Thursday before the opening of fishing season–Tuesday after Columbus Day

SITES: 44

EACH SITE: Picnic table, fire ring

ASSIGNMENT: First come, first served

REGISTRATION: Attendant will come by to register you

FACILITIES: Vault toilets, pump wells

PARKING: At campsites only

FEE: Wisconsin residents, $16; nonresidents, $21; plus vehicle admission fee (Wisconsin residents, $8; nonresidents, $11; Wisconsin residents age 65 and older, $3)

ELEVATION: 1,650'

RESTRICTIONS:

PETS: On leash only

FIRES: In fire ring only; firewood must be purchased in state within 10 miles of campground

ALCOHOL: At campsites only

VEHICLES: No restrictions

OTHER: 21-day stay limit

---

the least used and have much shade and privacy. Campsite 36 is in its own little world. Campsite 38 rests atop a hill. Campsite 39 overlooks the lake from its vantage point. The loop drops toward the lake and reaches sites 40, 42, and 44, each one big and facing toward Starrett Lake. The sites on the inside of this loop are used less.

Families and other campers return year after year to Starrett Lake. The campground usually fills on summer holiday weekends, but it often has open slots on other summer weekends. Friday arrivals are very likely to grab a site; I stayed here on a Friday in July, and many sites remained open. The facilities, including three pump wells and three bathrooms, are spread evenly throughout the camping area.

Stop by the Corner Store for a postride ice cream. *photographed by Mary Debilzen*

Hot showers are available at Crystal Lake and Firefly Campgrounds. Mountain bikers will be happy to learn about the Razorback Ridges trail system, which is developed and maintained by the Saynor–Star Lake Lions Club. The single- and doubletrack paths make numerous loops of varied difficulty. This trail system starts at the Saynor–Star Lake Lions Club trailhead, just down from the Corner Store on Razorback Road. In addition, an exceptional 53-mile paved bike path, Vilas County Bike the Heart Trail System, can be accessed across the road from the Corner Store. Bike rentals, as well as kayak and paddleboard rentals, are available at the Corner Store. You'll also find treats such as ice cream, refreshments, and camping and fishing supplies. Maps of both trail systems are also available at the Corner Store.

Water recreation is the name of the game here, but leave that gas motor behind. Consider bringing your canoe, kayak, or a rowboat to explore the 66-acre Starrett Lake. Self-propelled craft can easily cover the water surface, and anglers will find northern pike, walleye, and panfish in decent numbers. Largemouth bass are abundant, while smallmouth bass live here in fewer numbers. Campers can leave their boats by the small dock at the landing, while lakefront campers pull their boats up to their sites. The cove also has a beach area. Kids can be found horsing around in the lake, while adults float on rafts. A second water-access area lies across the cove near campsites 31–33.

Starrett Lake Campground

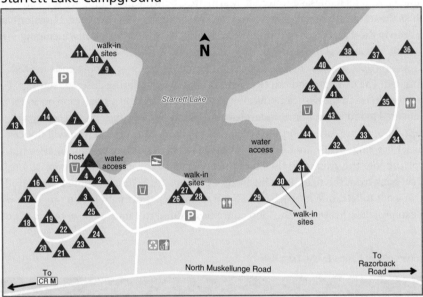

GETTING THERE

From the intersection of US 51 and WI 47 in Woodruff, head north on US 51 for 6.2 miles to County Road M. Turn right on CR M and follow it 2.7 miles to CR N. Turn right on CR N and follow it 4.9 miles to Razorback Road, near the Corner Store. Turn left on Razorback Road and follow it 1 mile to Big Muskellunge Lake Road. Turn left on Big Muskellunge Lake Road and follow it 1.8 miles to the campground on your right.

GPS COORDINATES: N46° 01.440' W89° 34.524'

49

Twelve Foot Falls Park Campground

Beauty ★★★★ / Privacy ★★★★ / Spaciousness ★★★★ / Quiet ★★★★★ / Security ★★★ / Cleanliness ★★★★

This waterfall-side campground is rustic and secluded.

Forget the roar of automobiles—the only roar you'll hear at this out-of-the-way campground is from its namesake waterfall. Marinette County, where this park is located, touts itself as the waterfall capital of Wisconsin. I have to agree. No fewer than 14 major named falls drop in the watersheds of this forestland, and five of these waterfalls, including Twelve Foot Falls, are in close proximity to this campground.

You won't see any RVs here; campers with holding tanks—camping code for RVs—are prohibited! The campground has two distinct areas, each offering different settings. Pass a pump well to reach the first camping area on the left, located on a small loop on an elevated flat covered in red pines. Some undergrowth separates these large and level campsites, and except for 5, all are located on the outside of the loop. At every site you will notice some unusual fire rings. They are circular and metal—that is nothing extraordinary—but they are placed into the ground so the lip of the fire ring is at ground level. Campsite 1 is large and set back from the road. Pass the next two campsites before reaching a short trail to a pair of vault toilets, one for each sex. Come to another short path leading to a site where you can purchase firewood. The loop continues around to campsite 4, large and set off by

Campers gather beside Twelve Foot Falls.

photographed by Kevin Revolinski

KEY INFORMATION

CONTACT: Marinette County, 715-732-7530, tinyurl.com/12footfalls

OPEN: May–November

SITES: 11

EACH SITE: Picnic table, in-ground fire ring

ASSIGNMENT: By phone; internet; or first come, first served

REGISTRATION: Self-registration on-site

FACILITIES: Vault toilet, pump well

PARKING: At campsites only

FEE: $15; $10 reservation fee

ELEVATION: 1,000'

RESTRICTIONS:

PETS: On leash only

FIRES: In fire ring only

ALCOHOL: No consumption of alcohol 1–4 a.m.

VEHICLES: 2/site

OTHER: Pack it in; pack it out

itself. Campsite 5 is the only undesirable site in the whole campground. The final two sites, 6 and 7, are well shaded in the pines with the help of a few oak trees.

To reach the second part of the campground, continue along the main road, which drops off the escarpment into a day-use area. Twelve Foot Falls comes into view. Look for a narrow, gravel road leading right to the lower campground, less than 100 feet from the North Fork Pike River. The roar of Twelve Foot Falls is louder down here. This small loop is dominated by evergreens growing thickly together. Campsite 8 is the most popular in the park because it is closest to the falls. The loop continues around to reach campsite 10, which has a side trail leading directly to the river. Campsite 12, the last, is all alone. A pair of vault toilets for each sex is located on the hill away from the river.

The first order of business is to take the trails to the falls. The trail to the right as you face the falls goes a short distance to a rock outcrop. Here you'll see the North Fork Pike River as it pours over a granite ledge into a large, swirling pool in its quest to meet the Menominee River to the east. To your right, the river again gathers steam and rushes around an island, working toward more waterfalls downstream. Across the water, Twelve Foot Falls—dark copper water of the North Fork Pike River—spills over a gray granite rampart in a frame of trees. The outcrop on which you stand makes for a great place to fish and a good place to drown—don't swim below the falls! The trail leading left as you face Twelve Foot Falls bridges a stream and works around to the head of the falls, where you can stand close to the rushing water and overlook the waterfall's pool. Informal trails continue both upriver and downriver for trout and pike fishing possibilities and to view a smaller falls just downriver.

Falls viewing and fishing are the two obvious camp-side activities. Twelve Foot Falls isn't one of those places where all the fun is laid out for you. You have to create your own action. If you are smart enough not to swim in the falls pool but still want to take a dip, head to Lily Lake. You passed it on the way in. This quiet lake has a roped-off swim beach with a convenient changing station. You can also execute a falls-viewing tour of Marinette County. Make sure to upload a county forest recreation map from the county website, or get one at the ranger station in Pembine. The map shows all the falls. You passed the side road to Eighteen Foot Falls on the way in. Horseshoe Falls is just a few miles from Twelve

Foot Falls, as are Carney Rapids and Four Foot Falls. Then you can return to Twelve Foot Falls and be sung to sleep by its white noise.

Twelve Foot Falls Park Campground

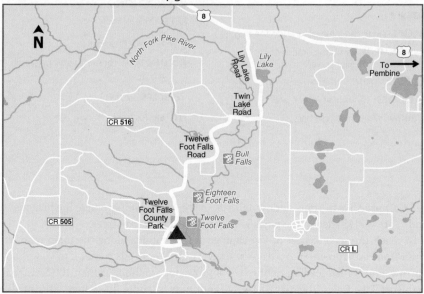

GETTING THERE

From the intersection of US 8 and US 141 near Pembine, head west on US 8 for 8 miles to Lily Lake Road. Turn left on Lily Lake Road and follow it 1.6 miles to Twin Lake Road. Turn right on Twin Lake Road and follow it 0.4 mile to Twelve Foot Falls Road. Turn left on Twelve Foot Falls Road and follow it 2.7 miles to the campground, on your left.

GPS COORDINATES: N45° 34.800' W88° 8.211'

50

Twin Lakes Campground

Beauty ★★★★★ / Privacy ★★★★★ / Spaciousness ★★★★ / Quiet ★★★★★ / Security ★★★ / Cleanliness ★★★★

Twin Lakes is very appealing, and so is the adjacent Round Lake Nonmotorized Area.

Maybe it was the cobalt-blue skies and the sunshine of the beautiful day, but Twin Lakes Campground shone during my camping trip there. The mixed forest of pines, evergreens, and hardwoods was deep green, the bark of paper birches glowing white. Twin Lake reflected the forest across the placid waters. I set up camp, promising to wet a line later, and headed just across Forest Road 142 to the Round Lake Nonmotorized Area. Here, a network of trails, open to both hikers and bikers, beckoned.

This campground is a true-blue winner. Campers who discover Twin Lakes end up returning year after year. Twin Lake is off to your left as you pass the boat launch and enter the campground, set on a brow overlooking the water. The campground road divides the camping area into two distinct groups. The sites to the left of the campground road—those that overlook the lake—are large, open in the center, and surrounded by tall trees such as red pines, maples, and birches that obscure all but the noonday sun. Spruces, firs, and brush grow between and among the campsites, which all have views of Twin Lake. Evergreen needles, gravel, and grass lie at the campsite floor. Campsite 17 is large and overlooks the lake. The most coveted site is 8, which lies all by itself at the end of a small auto turnaround.

The sites to the right of the road are smaller and are heavily shaded by evergreens and hardwoods. They literally look as though they were cut out of the forest. Heavy vegetation

A walkway leads down to Twin Lake.

courtesy of the U.S. Forest Service/public domain

KEY INFORMATION

CONTACT: Chequamegon-Nicolet National Forest Headquarters Offices, 715-362-1300, www.fs.usda.gov/cnnf; reservations 877-444-6777, recreation.gov

OPEN: May–October

SITES: 17

EACH SITE: Picnic table, fire grate

ASSIGNMENT: By phone; internet; or first come, first served

REGISTRATION: Self-registration on-site

FACILITIES: Vault toilet, water spigot

PARKING: At campsites only

FEE: $15

ELEVATION: 1,600'

RESTRICTIONS:

PETS: On leash only

FIRES: In fire ring only; firewood must be purchased in state within 10 miles of campground

ALCOHOL: At campsites only

VEHICLES: No restrictions

OTHER: 14-day stay limit

screens the sites, many of which are far back from the paved campground road. Campsites 1 and 2 exemplify these characteristics to the maximum. A grassy path runs behind many of the campsites here, and some are reservable (sites 5–11). Of these, the more secluded sites include 5–7. The water pump here is solar powered, so all you have to do is turn the faucet to get good aqua.

Twin Lake offers good fishing for largemouth bass on its 19 acres. Also sought are crappie, perch, and panfish. A short path near campsite 8 leads down to a small nonfishable lake. In my opinion, this unnamed small lake doesn't resemble Twin Lake. Two other lakes within short driving distance are Emily Lake and Wabasso Lake. Emily Lake, which has a fine campground of its own, has northern pike and panfish in its 26 acres. Wabasso Lake is bigger and contains bass, northern pike, and panfish.

The 3,600-acre Round Lake Nonmotorized Area is detailed in a map at the campground kiosk. Better yet, download one beforehand. The area is reached by foot from the trail just across from the campground road entrance. You can enjoy hiking or biking past prime waterfowl habitats, open fields, and thick woods, or take a trail to Round Lake. An alluring but narrow gravel beach lines the north shore of Round Lake. Old-growth hemlocks shade the forest floor between Round Lake and Tucker Lake. Little metal maps on signs can be found at each trail intersection. I saw a fisherman, beavers, and many birds on my hike. Bikers should be aware that the trails are grassy, and the grass can get high in summer.

Round Lake is the origin of the Flambeau River. A historic logging dam on Round Lake, built in 1878, has been restored; it is located on the way to Twin Lakes Campground. Back in the 1800s, Round Lake was filled with felled white pine logs, the dam gates were lowered, and off the logs went, destined for mills on the Chippewa and Mississippi Rivers. An interpretive trail crosses the dam and circles around the South Fork Flambeau River. You could hike to the dam from Twin Lakes Campground, but consider driving and save your hikes from the campground for the nonmotorized area. Round Lake has a boat launch and fishing opportunities too. Give yourself an opportunity to visit Twin Lakes and all it has to offer.

Twin Lakes Campground

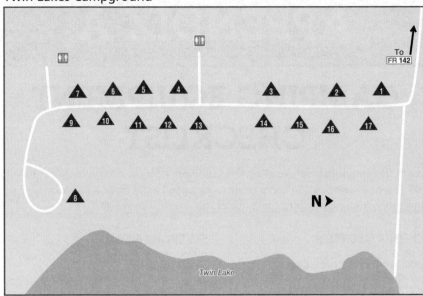

GETTING THERE

From the intersection of WI 13 and WI 70 in Fifield, drive east on WI 70 for 16.5 miles to Forest Road 144. Turn left on FR 144 and follow it 5.9 miles to FR 142. Turn right on FR 142 and follow it 2.3 miles to the campground, on your left.

GPS COORDINATES: N45° 57.376' W90° 4.294'

APPENDIX A

CAMPING EQUIPMENT CHECKLIST

Except for the large and bulky items on this list, I keep a plastic storage container full of the essentials for car camping so they're ready to go when I am. I make a last-minute check of the inventory, resupply anything that's low or missing, and away I go!

COOKING UTENSILS
Bottle opener
Bottles of salt, pepper, spices, sugar,
    cooking oil, and maple syrup in
    waterproof, spillproof containers
Can opener
Cups, plastic or tin
Dish soap (biodegradable), sponge, and towel
Flatware
Food of your choice
Frying pan
Fuel for stove
Lighter and/or matches in waterproof container
Plates
Pocketknife
Pot with lid
Stove
Tinfoil
Wooden spoon

FIRST AID KIT
Adhesive bandages
Aspirin
First-aid cream
Gauze pads
Insect repellent
Moleskin
Snakebite kit
Sunscreen/lip balm
Tape, waterproof adhesive

SLEEPING GEAR
Pillow
Sleeping bag
Sleeping pad, inflatable or insulated
Tent with ground tarp and rainfly

MISCELLANEOUS
Bath soap (biodegradable), washcloth, and towel
Camp chair
Candles
Cooler
Deck of cards
Flashlight with fresh batteries
Lantern
Maps (road, topographic, trails, and so on)
Paper towels
Plastic zip-top bags
Sunglasses
Toilet paper
Water bottle
Wool blanket

OPTIONAL
Barbecue grill
Binoculars
Field guides on bird, plant, and
    wildlife identification
Fishing rod and tackle
GPS

APPENDIX B

SOURCES OF INFORMATION

CHEQUAMEGON-NICOLET
NATIONAL FOREST
715-362-1300
www.fs.usda.gov/cnnf

WISCONSIN DEPARTMENT
OF TOURISM
800-432-8747
travelwisconsin.com

WISCONSIN STATE PARK SYSTEM
DEPARTMENT OF NATURAL RESOURCES
    BUREAU OF PARKS AND RECREATION
608-266-2621
dnr.wi.gov/topic/parks

INDEX

ABOUT THE AUTHORS

Kevin Revolinski was born and raised in Marshfield, Wisconsin. As a child he was fascinated by the Northwoods and Lake Superior whenever he visited his grandparents in Ashland. He is also the author of *The Yogurt Man Cometh: Tales of an American Teacher in Turkey*, *60 Hikes within 60 Miles: Madison*, and *Wisconsin's Best Beer Guide*. He has written for Rough Guides guidebooks, and his articles and photography have appeared in a variety of publications, including the *Chicago Tribune*, the *Wisconsin State Journal*, and the *Miami Herald*. He has lived abroad in several places, including Italy, Guatemala, and Panama, but he currently makes camp back in the homeland in Madison, Wisconsin. He maintains a travel website and accompanying blog at themadtraveler.com.

photographed by Preamtip Satasuk

photographed by Keri Anne Molloy

Johnny Molloy is an outdoors writer based in Johnson City, Tennessee. Born in Memphis, he moved to Knoxville in 1980 to attend the University of Tennessee (UT). During his college years, he developed a love of the natural world that has since become the primary focus of his life.

It all started on a backpacking foray into the Great Smoky Mountains National Park. That first trip was a disaster; nevertheless, Johnny discovered an affinity for the outdoors that would lead him to backpack and canoe-camp throughout the United States over the next three decades. Today, he averages nearly 200 nights out per year.

After graduating from UT with a degree in economics, Johnny spent an ever-increasing amount of time in the wild, becoming more skilled in a variety of environments. Friends enjoyed his adventure stories; one even suggested that he write a book. He pursued that idea and soon parlayed his love of the outdoors into an occupation.

The results of his efforts are more than 50 books. These include hiking, camping, paddling, and other comprehensive guidebooks, as well as books on true outdoor adventures. Johnny has also written for numerous publications and websites, as well as his local paper, the *Johnson City Press*. He continues to write and travel extensively to all four corners of the United States, exploring a variety of outdoor activities. For the latest on Johnny, please visit JohnnyMolloy.com.

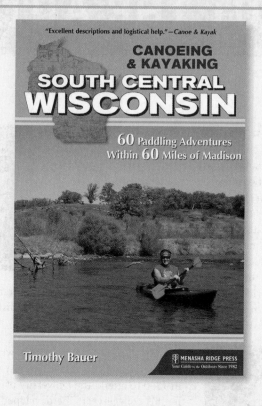

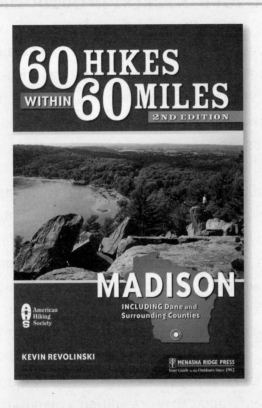

DEAR CUSTOMERS AND FRIENDS,

SUPPORTING YOUR INTEREST IN OUTDOOR ADVENTURE, travel, and an active lifestyle is central to our operations, from the authors we choose to the locations we detail to the way we design our books. Menasha Ridge Press was incorporated in 1982 by a group of veteran outdoorsmen and professional outfitters. For many years now, we've specialized in creating books that benefit the outdoors enthusiast.

Almost immediately, Menasha Ridge Press earned a reputation for revolutionizing outdoors- and travel-guidebook publishing. For such activities as canoeing, kayaking, hiking, backpacking, and mountain biking, we established new standards of quality that transformed the whole genre, resulting in outdoor-recreation guides of great sophistication and solid content. Menasha Ridge Press continues to be outdoor publishing's greatest innovator.

The folks at Menasha Ridge Press are as at home on a whitewater river or mountain trail as they are editing a manuscript. The books we build for you are the best they can be, because we're responding to your needs. Plus, we use and depend on them ourselves.

We look forward to seeing you on the river or the trail. If you'd like to contact us directly, visit us at menasharidge.com. We thank you for your interest in our books and the natural world around us all.

SAFE TRAVELS,

Bob Sehlinger

BOB SEHLINGER
PUBLISHER